STAR STRUCK

Messages from famous
people in the afterlife

KERRIE ERWIN

Title: *Star Struck – Messages from famous people in the afterlife*
Author: Kerrie Erwin
Copyright © 2026 Kerrie Erwin
Published in 2026 by Kerrie Erwin
Contact: www.pureview.com.au

PRINT ISBN: 9781763606524
EPUB ISBN: 9781763606531
Subjects: Spirituality | Self-help
Book Production: www.smartwomenpublish.com
Registered with the National Library Australia

All rights reserved. Except as permitted under the Australian Copyright Act 1968, no part of this book may be reproduced or transmitted in any form or by any means, electronic or mechanical, including photocopying, recording, scanning or information storage and retrieval system without the prior written consent of the publisher. No part of this book may be used by other parties without the author's prior written consent, for reproducing, publishing, communicating, or otherwise using the Work or any part of the Work to develop, train or direct Generative Artificial Intelligence technology or models ('Generative AI'), including but not limited to the mining or scraping of text, images or data from the Work.

Disclaimer

This book is a work of non-fiction, presented from a spiritual and metaphysical perspective. The accounts and messages described herein are the result of intuitive or mediumistic channelling conducted by the author over many years. While every effort has been made to portray the information faithfully, as received, readers are advised that such material reflects subjective spiritual impressions and should not be interpreted as verified historical.

The names of well-known individuals, including public figures and deceased celebrities, are used solely for the purpose of artistic, spiritual and educational exploration. The author makes no claim of factual or biographical accuracy regarding any communication attributed to these individuals. Any resemblance between the channelled content and actual events, persons or statements is coincidental or based on publicly available information.

This book is not intended as a substitute for professional advice in any field, nor does it purport to represent the official views, beliefs or intentions of the persons named or their estates. Readers are encouraged to approach the material with discernment and an open mind.

*'The spirit does not die when the body dies.
It is eternal and indestructible.'*

—Silver Birch

CONTENTS

Preface 1
Introduction 3
    What Happens When We Die 5
    Universal Messages from Famous Spirits 7
    Séances and the Gift of Spirit 8

PART ONE:
OPENING THE CIRCLE - A PRACTICAL GUIDE

1 The Importance of Protection with Spiritual Work 13
    White Light: The Ultimate Protection 14
    Different Ways of Protecting Ourselves 15
    White Light Protection Visualisation 18
    Creating the Space 19
    Spiritual Classes 20
    Clearing the Aura and Closing Your Chakras for Energy Work . 22

2 How to Meet and Work with Your Guide from the Light . . . 25
    How to Meet Your Guide in Meditation 26

3 Meet the Spirit Team 29
    Who are My Guides? 31

4 Meet My Star Seed Guides 39
   Star Seed Guides I have Channelled *40*
   Healing Symbols I have Received *44*
   The Cancer Symbol *44*
   The Arthritis Symbol *45*
   The Clearing, or Detox, Symbol *46*

5 Séances and Mediumship 47
   What is Physical Mediumship? *47*
   What is Trance Mediumship? *48*
   What is Transfiguration Mediumship? *49*
   Physical Mediumship and Séances *49*

6 Running My Own Home Circle 51
   The Benefits of Working as a Psychical Medium *53*

7 Conducting Séances: A Complete Guide 55
   Getting Started with Séance Work *55*
   Preparing for a Séance: What to Wear and Bring *56*
   Setting Up the Séance Room *56*
   Using Red and Blue Lights *57*
   Rules and Respect for Sacred Space *58*
   Protection: Opening and Closing Prayers *59*
   Working with Spirit and Group Energy *59*
   The Séance Process: Step by Step *60*
   Types of Phenomena You May Experience *61*
   Spirit Healing During Séances *62*
   Closing the Séance *63*
   My Personal Experience with Séances *64*
   Famous Spirits Coming Through *64*
   Closing the Circle – When Spirit Calls Time *66*

8 Unexpected Famous Spirit Guests 69

PART TWO: STARS AND CELEBRITIES

Muhammad Ali	74	Val Kilmer	149
Lauren Bacall	76	Vivien Leigh	152
Tammy Faye Baker	78	John Lennon	154
Lucille Ball	80	Little Richard	157
Jeff Beck	84	Christine McVie	160
John Belushi	86	Jayne Mansfield	163
Marlon Brando	89	Jim Morrison	166
Karen Carpenter	92	Bert Newton	169
Sir Sean Connery	95	Dame Olivia Newton-John	172
Miles Davis	98	Sinead O'Connor	174
Sammy Davis Jr	100	Lisa Marie Presley	177
John Denver	103	Princess Margaret	179
Marlene Dietrich	106	Queen Elizabeth II	181
Harry Edwards	109	Helen Reddy	183
Farrah Fawcett	112	Christopher Reeve	185
Roberta Flack	115	Debbie Reynolds	188
Aretha Franklin	118	Alan Rickman	191
Clark Gable	121	Mickey Rooney	193
George Harrison	124	Bon Scott	196
Jimi Hendrix	127	Frank Sinatra	198
Katharine Hepburn	129	Anna Nicole Smith	201
Philip Seymour Hoffman	132	Doris Stokes	204
Bob Hope	135	Gloria Swanson	207
Barry Humphries	138	Tina Turner	210
Marc Hunter	141	Paul Walker	213
Michael Jackson	143	Shane Warne	215
Janis Joplin	145	Dame Vivienne Westwood	217
Jack Kerouac	147	Betty White	220

Conclusion – The Medium in a Modern World 223

Afterword 225

Recommended Reading 227

About the Author 229

PREFACE

Beloved friends. This book is a sacred record of the private and closed séances I held with my sitters over a period of 18 years. While most of the spirits came through in the group energy or the séance room, I also had some come to me in my own meditation room at home, at various times. Perhaps they wanted to be in the book as well, as there certainly was a flurry of energy while writing this book.

My intention in writing *Starstruck* is to give a beautiful tribute to the stars of yesteryear, with love and gratitude. To the many wonderful spirits and souls who came through, delivering messages of love, personal insights, and inspiration, we salute you and thank you ever so kindly.

The message I keep getting, and which I send to you today, is that anything is possible when working with the spirit world. There are always new spiritual lessons and valuable teachings to learn. My mantra is– no matter what knowledge you already have, or think you have, you never know it all, so it's always good to keep an open mind when working with the spirit world.

I have been a devoted student for many years, and through my work I have come to understand the spirit world I speak of is a vast, incredible consciousness of love, light and healing. It's also an uncharted dimension, as yet undiscovered by us mere mortals.

My gift to you is simply to pass along these timely messages of encouragement, hope and love to help you build a far better world on a personal level. The many souls within these pages tell how they did it, with success, when they were alive. It's not about earthbound souls, confused and lost in a cold, grey world called the astral, who need assistance with crossing over with spirit rescue. It's about souls who have safely crossed, had their life review, completed their healing and spiritual contracts here on Earth, and are ready for reincarnation.

The amazing messages from well-known icons who once walked on Earth offer inspiration and hope to every single one of us, from all walks of life, with the main purpose of developing our spiritual awakening and belief in ourselves. The messages that came through the medium varied: some were long, while others were just a few words. The intention that came through was solely– let light and love be your guide to a better world.

It is my belief the spirit world, and those loving beings who reside on the other side—such as our own loved ones, spiritual guides and powerful angels—are our allies, and work with us to create balance and calm in the universe, helping us to live happier and more inspiring lives. With all the political unrest, useless and cruel wars, countless refugees, new technologies and other global issues, such as climate change causing irreversible damage to the planet, these messages are timely as we go to a new level of consciousness in our world.

As we light a candle, let us give thanks and gratitude to spirit from the bottom of our hearts for the much-needed guidance and help we constantly receive in our daily lives.

On a personal level, my gift to you today is a reminder to love yourself, stay focused and always believe in yourself, no matter the odds, as dreams can come true.

Blessings and love
Kerrie Erwin X

INTRODUCTION

As far as I can remember, I have always been psychic and a natural medium. I was just born this way. I have always been able to communicate with living spirits who have crossed safely, and the earthbound spirits I help with my rescue team of devoted guides.

When I was in my early twenties, I received a download while travelling overseas. I had a near-death experience after a freak accident. As I was pulled out of my body with incredible speed and force, I looked below and saw myself lying limply on the busy street, with people screaming and yelling all around me. I was aware of what was going on, but it happened so fast that I didn't care.

The pulling sensations lasted for a while, then I saw myself floating way above my body. The next thing I knew, I was flying at a swift pace, past everything I had ever known—the sky, the clouds, the earth—until finally I reached space. Once there, I flew past the stars and planets, which looked like beacons of bright light on a black canvas, until I arrived in what I can only describe as a vast, bottomless void full of pure white, blinding light, which felt very welcoming and warm.

The energy I experienced was nothing like the energy here on Earth. The feelings I experienced were strange; I felt comfort with all of this. It was as if I'd entered a type of multiverse, where everything felt peaceful and right, as if all the energy and particles were directly pieced together and connected. A high consciousness of all-loving and totally consuming energy reigned supreme. For me, the pure, blinding, unconditional love and light were totally overwhelming.

I don't remember much after that, as, within what seemed like seconds, I was somewhere else and quickly brought back into my body, which was aching after losing consciousness due to my accident. All I could hear was a friend calling my name, who I could see was by my side when I opened my eyes.

Once I'd landed back in my body, I felt incredibly calm about everything. It was as if I had died, found purpose, and had come back to have another go. Little did I know this had all happened for a reason: to really set me on my path. The pain was unbearable, but a strong, reassuring voice, screaming loudly within my head, told me I would be okay, and I would soon be back to my normal self. This voice was my higher self.

My life was certainly not normal after that, but the experience seemed to give me a reality check on who I was and what I was meant to do through service, for spirit, with my psychic gifts.

From my many sessions with spirit people as a medium, past-life regression, séances, and mental mediumship with my spirit team, I have come to understand that the spirit world is a vast consciousness of love, light, and healing. To some people, it can seem like a place in nature, or a great city, or another place holding good memories. Over the years, my guides have told me the spirit world is just an arm's length away, but in another dimension.

As a spiritualist, I believe it's a good thing to know that when you die, there is no ending. Instead, there's a transition to another plane, which is not only brighter and lighter than the world you have known but also takes you to a higher consciousness. Writing this book reminded me of that. I also know, through my many mediumship sessions, that love is eternal and never ends.

What Happens When We Die

Death. It's shrouded in mystery. Feared by many. It's no wonder people are curious: it's the oldest mystery of all, something beyond the reach of scientific investigation or technological advancement. It is difficult to understand, even after being explained by those who have died for a couple of minutes and come back. It's also something I'm happy to share my knowledge about, and I hope by sharing, I can alleviate some of that fear, both for your loved ones and for yourself, when the time comes.

While feared, death is simply a step in your journey. You do not actually die. You are not your body; it is just the shell that contains your soul. So, when you die, you cast off your shell and return to your true form, crossing to the next stage of your journey.

This process, or transition, is called 'crossing over'. When you cross into heaven, which is in another dimension, the process is described as beautiful, providing the spirit with a sense of elation, and complete and total peace. Immediately, you are free of suffering. If you were ill before your death, you are no longer ill; if you were old and frail, you are no longer so.

All the spirits I have connected with in my work, and the many spirits I have connected with in sessions, have told me that once they cross into the spirit world, they actually feel young again, and in the prime of their lives.

Once you arrive with your guide, as a soul, you embark on a spiritual journey, which includes reuniting with soulmates, spirit guides and loved ones, souls that are on your vibrational level. People who have done the afterlife work, or had near-death experiences, often say it's a busy place. In fact, it is an uncharted, living and colourful world, full of a large menagerie of highly evolved, loving beings and master spirits, including a hierarchy of angels, powerful archangels, and spiritual guides. They are there as spirit helpers to assist you with your human journey. They are ascended master energies and your own loved ones who have crossed safely to the other side and are connected to you eternally through their love.

After we die and cross over into the spirit world, as spirits, we receive a *life review*, during which we spend time assessing the many lessons we learned while on Earth, with higher beings guiding us through this process. As spirits, we also receive healing from the place of oneness, a place of pure, unconditional love, where we are returned to our true soul essence. Through this process, we learn about our life's journey, which helps us raise our vibration and deepen our spiritual growth.

Most of us have gone through the loss of someone we care about, and it's an experience that stays with us forever. It is comforting, then, to know our loved ones in the spirit world remain connected to us through their eternal love. They do this through mediums, dreams and often spirit signs, or just a sense of *knowing* our loved ones are around us. An example of this, from one of my clients, is:

> *I have been dating this most amazing man, and I was about to lend him a lot of money. The weird thing is, the day before I was to go to the bank, I had a nightmare, with my late dad telling me no, no, no. When I woke up in the morning, I knew Dad was around as I could smell his aftershave lingering in the room. Lucky for me, I dumped the man straight away and found out later that he was married and using a fake name. It was so real I nearly fainted.*

I also like to share that before we incarnated and lived our lives on Earth, we chose our parents; we chose to reconnect with our soul family, which we usually incarnate with each time we return to learn new lessons. We know the struggles we'll face in human form, which are lessons to learn. We also know how long we will spend learning our lessons each time we incarnate. We make these choices.

Universal Messages from Famous Spirits

I have always been dedicated to my spiritual work and have told spirit many times my intention is to learn as much as I can, to help people. As our intentions are in alignment with the law of attraction, which connects to our emotions, I am always given opportunities to fulfil my wishes.

Imagine my surprise when, after many years of sittings in my private séances called the 'golden circle of light', with loved ones and pets coming through from the spirit world, I started to bring forward celebrities and famous icons we had all known here on Earth and once loved. We had grown up with some of them, and here they were, telling their stories in my small group in the suburbs.

I could not believe what was happening. I was meeting so many remarkable and talented people. It seemed as if the group energy had a life of its own, governed by spirit, so we just went with it. I have to say, it was not only remarkable, but also very entertaining talking to famous icons, in spirit, who had once walked amongst us.

The stories and insight were all the same: messages of encouragement, wisdom and love. The most amazing thing was they were all happy to share the lessons they had learnt on their own spiritual journeys.

In one way, I wasn't surprised by this intervention and sudden change, as most of us in my small group were like-minded; we either had musical backgrounds, had worked in the entertainment industry, or had other artistic connections. As for me, I have a history of playing bass guitar in several bands, working in film and television, and touring with stage shows all over Australia, so it made sense that Hollywood had come to my home circle, to show us how they did it all their way.

Séances and the Gift of Spirit

After a while, the group energy in the séances I had worked as medium and leader for many years, began to change at a fast pace, taking on a new and exciting energy of its own, which was different from anything I had ever experienced. Since it was an experimental group, setup under strong guidelines, I had no expectations and just went with it. Over the years, I have come to know that my mediumship is a work in progress, so I just trust in the process. spirit will always take me where I need to go for the learning experience and its many rewards.

Feeling over the moon, I was so excited to be a channel, to receive so much insight and information from these famous people who had crossed safely into the spirit world, all wanting to bring through information with stories of their own experiences, for the good of humanity. I was receiving so much information about people I not only loved but had followed throughout my life.

After each session, when the group energy had been closed down with a prayer by the head sitter, or control, and I was once again back in my body, we would always thank the spirit team. We also made a point of researching the information when we went home to see if it was correct. When it was time to leave, we would all still be high, full of energy, as if we had attended a party. I still remember the joy and merriment from those nights and later would smile and giggle when I remembered all the laughter and yelling from the group sitters, when someone famous came in to join us.

The messages in those sessions were always the same; they were always about the fragility of the human spirit, and how everyone was the same, no matter how famous they were. We all have lessons and learning, trials and tribulations with our spiritual contacts, except these words of wisdom were from famous people who had each worked hard and made it to the top in their chosen field.

It was amazing to think every single one of them wanted not only to be remembered, but also to give us healing, inspiration and love, in the hope, I guess, we would spread the word of love to everyone we knew.

PART ONE

OPENING THE CIRCLE

A PRACTICAL GUIDE

Part One focuses on information about spiritual practices, séances, and mediumship. It's a practical how-to guide for working with the spirit world in a protected and safe manner.

1
THE IMPORTANCE OF PROTECTION WITH SPIRITUAL WORK

As a practising spiritualist, a person who believes that the spirits of the dead can communicate with the living, I believe death as we know it is not an ending. It is a welcome transition back home into the spirit world, another dimension, which is just an arm's length away. I believe once we have completed our spiritual contracts here on Earth, we return to the higher realms of what is called the *spirit world* for reincarnation and completing another cycle.

The spirit world I refer to is a higher plane of pure consciousness, enlightenment and divine connection, believed to be the source of all creation and universal truth in another dimension. In between Earth and the spirit world, where most of us cross, is another world, plane or realm called the astral. It's a cold, confusing, multilayered world in which lost souls, earthbound spirits and spirit creatures of legend are residing, expanding downward into the depths of primordial forces. In other words, it's not a good place. Most of these souls are lost and confused, and don't understand they're dead. This is because they're of a lower vibration and still attached to their old lives.

Some of the most fundamental things I learnt when starting out as a young medium were protection, boundaries and the importance of closing down my energy—grounding—at the end of meditation; working with spirits; and energy work with healing. We aim to work with benevolent spirits only, as sometimes we may be working in uncharted waters, where there may be trickster spirits who don't come from the light of love and consciousness. Also, this is not a game for people with ego to play, or a weapon to be used for gain. It's about respect when working with the spirit world.

We will always have our loving spirit team to protect us from unwanted energies from the astral or negative souls, but it's our own personal responsibility to look after ourselves. As sensitive souls, or natural empaths, who do the work, we need this protection as a second skin to stop any unwanted and toxic energy that may upset us.

White light is the ultimate loving energy; it's very simple, and anyone can use it, no matter their faith or religion, as it's pure, unconditional, universal love. It's gentle and positive, and when visualised and used, it provides the highest degree of spiritual protection against negative energies. It's the most powerful and the best protection in the world and can provide the greatest healing on so many levels. It is particularly important for empathic people, as it shields them from the effects of feeling others' emotions.

White Light: The Ultimate Protection

White light is made up of all the colours of the spectrum and is unconditional love in its highest form. Some describe it as 'electromagnetic energy of waves' – the most powerful tool in the universe. With its mixture of all colour frequencies, it gathers and stores all the positive energy and is far stronger than negative or dark energy. It also represents purity and divinity.

When I was younger, I was taught to wrap this energy around me, as a bubble of love, for protection, so nothing could hurt me, and to leave a night light on, because spirits can go wild in the dark. I remember using this as a child, so I wouldn't be jumped on or pulled out of bed in the middle of the night by unruly spirits just trying to get my attention or prove a point. When I used my protective bubble, I had a good night's sleep and didn't experience any terrifying nights. Out of habit, to this day, I still use my bubble of protection, and at night, I still use a night light and say an extra prayer.

Different Ways of Protecting Ourselves

In any type of spiritual work, always use white-light energy for protection by imagining it surrounding you as a protective barrier. You can also do this with your loved ones, ensuring that they – and their homes and possessions – remain safe. If you're going through tough times, as extra protection, try using gold light as well. To do this, in your mind's eye, imagine the energy as the sun, and wrap it around your body and aura, dissolving any darkness in its shadows.

White light energy is the main protection I use, but there are many other practices to strengthen your energy and stay safe.

- **Boundaries:** Always exercise strong boundaries with everyone in your life. When you take responsibility for yourself, your energy often shifts, and you won't be attracted to certain energy types. Make sure you set healthy boundaries to avoid feeling depleted by too many people taking your energy. Set goals and notice how quickly you can manifest them.

- **Intuition:** Listen to your intuition, as it's never wrong; it's often your higher self or soul energy talking to you. It may also be your guide stepping in and speaking as well. I don't know how many times I've heard people say they had a feeling something was wrong, or a thought went through their minds telling them the same thing. These moments of truth—the gut feelings and sense of knowing—are real and should be listened to. Sometimes your subconscious mind shows you answers in your dreams.

- **Diet:** Eat a balanced diet. Everything in moderation, and that includes alcohol. I never mix drugs or alcohol when working with spirit, nor do I allow people in my groups if they're taking drugs. Clean energy is essential.

- **Bathing:** If you're feeling drained, soak in a bath with Epsom salts to clear away negative energy and any debris you have collected from the aura. Make this a daily ritual.

- **Cloaking:** This is another way of protecting yourself. If you don't want to be noticed when walking into a room, or when you're out and about, pull in your aura and imagine you have an invisible cloak wrapped around you. This will pull in your energy, and you'll be able to walk around and mingle without attracting too much attention.

- **Saging:** Another way of clearing negative energy from your energy field is to burn a good sage stick and just wave it through your aura.

- **Music:** Drumming or playing any musical instrument yourself or listening to music can be very uplifting.

- **Meditation:** For at least twenty minutes a day, meditate and make positive affirmations. Also, make it a rule to always close all your chakras, or energy points, after working with people or meditating. This is a good way to protect yourself after a meditation, so you're not open to other people's energy or vibrations.

- **Laugh:** Have a good laugh and a catch-up with friends. It's great to have good friends in your life and help lift the load during difficult times.

- **Grounding:** Practise grounding exercises – walking, martial arts, gym, dancing, yoga or any other form of exercise – as this raises your energy and prevents you from feeling depleted.

Many students I have worked with over the years have struggled with being scattered and unable to grow spiritually or reach higher powers, all because they were not grounded in the earth.

- **Play:** Make time for fun in your life with friends and loved ones.
- **Friendship:** Release the 'poor-me' people from your life. Over time, you will often find that they're sucking your energy and wasting your time. I can't tell you how important this is. You need to have good friends, not just people who need you to help all the time.
- **Say no:** Saying no feels good, and it's a powerful thing to be able to do, especially if it's something you usually find hard.
- **Declutter:** Lose the clutter in your home. Anything that does not serve you is just blocking energy.
- **Self-love:** It's very important to learn to love yourself. If you don't, who else will?
- **Forgiveness:** This is the key to healing. Always be willing to forgive loved ones, friends, or anyone who has hurt you. You don't have to remain close; you can move away. When you walk the spiritual path, your journey in life will always be full of new learnings. Once you begin to work with your innate psychic powers, your energy will shift to a higher frequency, or level, which in turn will take you to a new karmic cycle, and people who no longer serve you will leave. This, of course, can be really hard. These painful lessons can take you off your path, disempower you, and hold you back from where you're meant to be, if you don't let go and move on. An easy way to let go is to place such people in a big pink bubble of healing love, forgive them, let them go, and surrender your pain to the angels. If people are meant to be in your life, they will be. Soulmates and companion souls will always stay around you.

White Light Protection Visualisation

Before working with spirit, surround yourself in white light for protection and balance.

1. Find a quiet space where you can be alone. Gently close your eyes and, taking three deep breaths in and out, ask spirit to surround you with white light. If you're using the white light for protection, envision it coming down over you and enveloping you in a protective bubble.
2. Once the white light surrounds you, state your intention. For example: 'Protect me from the negative energy I will encounter today.' There are many different mantras and chants available for you to use.
3. As you sit with your eyes closed, still breathing slowly and deeply, visualise the white light as it travels to each chakra in your body. Allow it to cleanse each chakra until you feel light and visualise it moving on to the next.
4. Surrounding yourself in white light like this will ensure that you aren't affected by people who are draining your energy. You know who they are.

The process for self-healing is just as simple, but instead of surrounding yourself with the white light, visualise the white light entering your body through the top of your head, and then flowing through your body, the same as the protective bubble.

This White-light visualisation can be used daily, helping you to feel balanced, calm and positive. It's good to use for loved ones, too, and property. With this ritual, I never worry about loved ones; I just place a white light around them daily and know they are always safe.

I will also close down my chakras after doing any type of work. You can do this easily by imagining your chakras like little lights closing down, one at a time.

And as I am so sensitive, I generally use a bubble of light daily. If the energy is really toxic, like a psychic attack, I will also wrap a dark blue cloak for added protection.

Creating the Space

In my experimental séances, I will always remove any clutter from the work room and only have a few toys or tools laying around for the session. Things like balls, or small squeaky toys, all fluorescent, that glow in the dark and can be used by the spirit people, including spirit children, to throw around for evidence of paranormal and spirit activity during the séance.

I don't like others to use the space I run my group in, as it's a sacred space and one I use solely for the séance. I've been very lucky to have had this opportunity, as I could never imagine sharing and blending my energies with those of others I don't know, and their residual energies. This simple rule also helps me build the energy, making it easier to connect with the spirits who come to visit.

The space I work in is easily darkened with some black curtains that keep the light out. I always clear the space beforehand, giving it a good smoking with some sage. This takes care of any residual energy that may be lingering, or by spirits who may have been left behind and not crossed over when asked. I also like to air out the space with fresh air before every sitting, something that's essential for me, because I'm very sensitive to energy and smells.

I make it a habit to work with the same dedicated sitters. I always know how many people are coming, as I don't welcome drop-ins who just want a bit of entertainment. This way I can prepare the exact number of chairs needed and arrange in a circle.

In the middle of the room, I have my small spinning table with the small silver trumpet on top; it has fluorescent tape around the edges, so it glows in the dark and is easy to watch for spiritual activity. In winter, the sitters are given small blankets, as it can get cold. Some mediums like to use a cabinet to sit apart from the sitters. However, as I don't like small spaces, I sit in a corner of the room in my comfortable lounge chair, away from the working circle of sitters, as I go under, into my trance state.

Spiritual Classes

Training is an integral part of the spiritual journey as you learn to work with grounding, protection and your own loving guides who will take you on the journey.

Anyone who wants to develop their spiritual gifts to help others, or just work on themselves, may find it easier to sit in a group and work with the energies. You will always have loving support and guidance from the teacher and the other sitters, plus a sense of belonging and a knowing you are not alone, and that others like you have gifts. Once you're on this path, you will have many teachers over the years, including your own guides.

I've sat in different energy and healing groups for years to learn my craft as a medium. For many years now, I have sat with my own guides, and my teachings have come through meditations. They can be very vivid, clear, informative, and extremely loving and helpful.

In my training and development days as a psychic medium in a small spiritualist church, we undertook a meditation with the teacher and travelled through many higher levels of consciousness until we met infinity, or what she described as a figure eight, which is the symbol for eternity.

After the exercise and a deep meditation, we were invited by the teacher to share our experience and openly discuss what we saw. As we went around the room, everybody said they saw types of angels and gave detailed descriptions of how fantastic it was.

One of the women was in awe and shared the only thing she saw were thousands and thousands of what looked like spaceships, fleets of them as far as the eye could see, in all shapes and sizes, as if they had come from a different galaxy, dimension or universe, joining together in some type of group or federation. To her, they felt like 'space angels'.

As soon as she said this, everyone went quiet, and the teacher, looking bewildered, burst out laughing, as if she felt the whole thing was hilarious. For me, this was a transformational moment. Honestly, I was confused and a little bit taken aback by the teacher's reaction. Everybody is different, and on their own unique spiritual journey, and I saw this as a weakness in the teacher. It seemed to me the so-called teacher was judgmental and projecting her own fears onto the class, while everybody else saw loads of light and angels everywhere.

The next time we had that class, the woman was not there, and not long after that, I left as well. I felt that the group had become stagnant, with too many rules.

A few months later, I joined another group, which was more progressive and was run by a wonderful teacher. The teacher, a wise and spiritual Native American, said it was an absolute honour to work with us. He said we were all constantly learning so many things, and it was an incredible world we lived in. His mantra was: 'There are always going to be different types of rewarding spiritual experiences, with countless possibilities in our undiscovered and forever changing world, and unexplored, unlimited universe.'

One thing I do know is with the spirit and human experience, we are constantly discovering new and exciting ideas and technologies. If we want growth in our lives, it's wise to keep an open mind and not judge others by our own learnings. Not everyone is going to have the same experience, and we learn by listening and being respectful of other people's truth.

After a couple of more years, and working with many teachers, I learnt my spiritual development would continue but would be with my own spiritual guides in meditation and trance. My spirit team, which is here to help me, has far more wisdom than any person on the planet. For this, I am truly grateful.

Clearing the Aura and Closing Your Chakras for Energy Work

A meditation for the white-room technique is an exercise for sensitive souls to undertake when doing any type of paranormal and energy work, as well as working in other dimensions. As I've share before I firmly believe it is important to close down all your chakras when doing energy work and ground yourself. The more grounded you are, the higher you can go.

1. Find a quiet place where you won't be disturbed or go to your sacred space and light a candle.
2. Once you are comfortable, sit up straight, and slowly breathe in and out deeply three times to release any stress or tightness from the body.
3. Now gently visualise yourself starting to bring healing energy up from the earth star into your base chakra. As you do this, feel it moving around your body. Begin to blow out any negative energy through your mouth with your breathing.
4. Continue this process, moving slowly upwards, making sure you continue to breathe out, releasing as you continue up through all your chakras: begin with base (red), sacral (orange), solar plexus (yellow), heart (green), throat (blue), third eye (indigo), crown (purple), and transpersonal point (white). As you do this, feel all your chakras gently align.
5. Now imagine yourself in a white room. As you do this with your eyes closed, look to the left and check if you sense or feel anything there. If so, ask it to leave and go into the light, or wherever it came from. If anything was there, once it has gone, proceed to the next side.
6. Now check your right side and do the same until that's clear as well.

7. Repeat with the back and front. Do this until there's nothing in the white room with you. The white room, which is your auric field, needs to be clear, and no attachments or clutter.
8. When you've done this, close down all your chakras or energy centres, as if they're little lights, and ground your energy to the earth. Open your eyes.
9. If you feel you need extra help, start having Epsom salt baths or swimming in the sea as this is also good for cleansing energy. If this is hard, get a spray bottle, make a mix with salt or Epsom salt, and spray the aura. Either will work.

2
HOW TO MEET AND WORK WITH YOUR GUIDE FROM THE LIGHT

Early on in my training, I was asked to identify the sources of the messages I conveyed to clients, aside from those communicated by loved ones in the spirit world. I am clairaudient, and I hear the messages so clearly in my head that it's like I'm speaking on a phone. I also have other gifts.

Being a natural psychic medium, I had no idea who the familiar voice offering guidance was until I meditated and worked in trance. Imagine my surprise when I saw a huge Native American spirit man, with a headdress on, sitting in front of me.

I soon learnt the best teachers you will have on the path of your spiritual development are your own loving guides and angels, who are with you from birth and stay with you until you die. Even though it might seem you're alone at times, that's never the case, even for a minute, because the love of spirit is always with you.

As we develop our spirituality, we're given different spiritual helpers and guides along the way. Angels will step in when asked, and of course, we have our loved ones in spirit, as love is eternal. Some guides will come and go. Our loved ones may move on in the spirit world or reincarnate, but our main guide will stay with us from birth to death and can be called on at any time for assistance and guidance. They will often work with us to move spiritually to another level or vibration, and then they may depart or step back. Along my path. I have worked in many different areas and with many different guides.

How to Meet Your Guide in Meditation

If you'd like to meet your guides as I have, begin with this simple meditation practice to create a safe and welcoming space for connection.

1. Find yourself a sacred space in your home.
2. Light a white candle and on the altar, place daisies, violets, or autumn leaves of many different colours, if available.
3. I love to work with crystals. Perhaps you would like to add some to your altar, too. Black obsidian can help dissolve anger, fear, and negativity. Rose quartz is for unconditional and divine love. Clear quartz crystals, or terminator crystals, help balance and energise the energy in the room and the chakras in the body. Kyanite is for psychic protection. When I work with crystal energy, I love the smell of mirth, lavender and rose.
4. When you're ready, gently take three deep breaths, in and out, until you begin to feel your body totally relax.
5. When you're ready, slowly count in your mind's eye backwards from ten to one.
6. Once you have done this, visualise in your mind's eye a beautiful place in nature.
7. As you relax more and more, feel the lovely warmth from the sun on your body, soft grass beneath your feet. You begin to feel relaxed and comfortable.
8. Now, using your imagination, smell the sweet scents of nature—flowers, trees, grass—all around you, as the gentle wind blows on your skin.

9. Once you feel one with everything around you, find a place to sit and rest.
10. When you're ready, gently breathe out three times and call in your loving guide from the light.
11. As you do this, you'll feel a presence. Ask if the guide comes from the light. Important note: If you get a 'no' response, tell the presence to leave and move back to where it came from. There are tricksters in the spirit world who come from a lower vibration and who like nothing better than to play games with you. (Your true guide, when asked, will not demand or tell you what to do, or misguide you in any way.) Once you have sent this negative presence away, keep calling for your guide from the light to come in. If this doesn't work, shut down the energy and try again later.
12. Now you have met the guide, feel the love and compassion that shows they are willing to work with you. Understand you are safe and secure, and no harm will come to you.
13. Once you have made contact, you will probably have many questions. You can begin by asking for a name or if they have a message. You can also ask for a spirit sign in your daily life, for instance, a feather, to show that all is well and you're being looked after.
14. Spend some time with your guide, and when you're ready to come back, thank them for coming through today.
15. When you're ready, gently close down all your energy centres, starting with the crown chakra at the top of the head, then work your way down to the third eye, throat, heart, solar plexus and sacral until you finally reach the base chakra. You can do this by imagining them closing down, like little lights, ever so gently, and then grounding your energy to the earth.
16. Now imagine, in your mind's eye, running white light through all your energy centres, or chakras, to remove any residual energy until you feel yourself back in your body. Once you have done this, wiggle your toes.

17. Open your eyes and thank your guide with great gratitude.
18. Understand that now you have made contact, you can talk to them any time; they will stand by your side. For example, my guide stands on the left side, and when I tilt my head, I can receive guidance for any problems.

3
MEET THE SPIRIT TEAM

When we are born, we come with our own team of spiritual guides, angel helpers and guardian angels. We have one main spiritual guide in mediumship, called the gatekeeper, who stays with us from birth to death. Throughout your development, other guides will come and go as you learn or study new things.

I will give you an example. I had always been interested in spiritual healing in my practice, so decided to study Reiki and many other forms of spiritual healing to help others. Before long, I was joined in meditation by a loving, healing guide who called himself Dr Lee. I learnt before he died, he had been a medical doctor while living on Earth. Every time I do any healing, I hear his voice in my ear, gently directing me and giving me instructions on where to place my hands on the client's body, and which energy or symbols to channel. With the assistance of this spirit guide, I'm also able to imagine a type of blueprint, or map, of the client's meridians, or energy centres. In my mind's eye, this enables me to see any type of blocked energy within the client's body that needs healing.

These days, I have between six and eight guides who come in and out of my life, but I have three prominent guides who are constantly working with me in my roles as a professional medium, teacher and writer.

When I trance channel, my main guide, the gentle Native American spirit chief called White Feather (who was once my father in one of my lifetimes) protects me. This gentle soul is what I call the gatekeeper, and his duty is to make sure unwanted or malevolent spirits do not come into my energy field or cause me any harm. Over the years, White Feather has moved to one side, but he is still always there.

These days, I mainly work with a very wise and powerful teacher called Romanov, who not only gives me direction but also helps me with all my work, including my readings, stage shows, and my ongoing work with the media.

When Romanov came in, I had been suffering from headaches for a while, which was a high-frequency thing, but I have now come to understand this was happening for a specific reason. There was a shift in my vibration as the new guide was very powerful.

Over the years, I've discovered that guides will often come and go. When we have finished working with them, they will let us know in meditation they are stepping aside to allow another guide, or guides, with a new vibration to come in to help with the spiritual journey. This helps with the progression of the soul.

Many people I have worked with, mostly students, have been visited by my guides, and quite often they tell me when they feel the guides' presence.

Our guide—our guardian or gatekeeper—is here to assist us with our everyday lives and spiritual contract on Earth. When we've finished our time on Earth, our loving guide returns with us to the spirit world. As the bond and love connection between the two is so strong, it may be understood as sharing a past life with this enlightened being.

Our guide is loving and caring, and may be a relative, friend or someone who has passed over to the spirit world and is now living in spirit. Until we pass over to join our guide as a spirit, they protect us from negative energies, staying with us throughout our lives and protecting our soul. When we nurture the bond between ourselves and our guide, the trust and natural relationship can develop into immense strength, which may help us through more challenging times in our lives.

We may also have many other guides throughout our lives, as well as angels come and watch over us. I practise trance mediumship, so I know who these guides are and what they can help me with. I decided to sit in a trance group to learn exactly who these guides were, especially since I was listening to and talking with them. When learning about my guides, although there are many stages of trance mediumship, I chose not to use a deep trance state, as I like to remember things. If you want to know more about your team spirit guides, you need to sit in a spiritual development circle, and over time, you will become very proficient.

I have seen angels when I work with past-life regression, as they often come in when people have experienced a tragic death in a past life. They are magnificent beings, but we need to call them in as they only come when we need them. When we have asked them for help, we need to thank them for their assistance, as well.

You need to remember, even though it may seem you are all alone at times, it is never the case. As with faith and a positive mindset, the love of spirit is always with you.

The various guides I have worked with, have helped me through difficult times with love, compassion and gentle coaching. Without this team of incredible beings, always assisting me, I would never have been able to do my work as a medium today. If ever I have any problems, I always ask for help, and it is soon on the way.

Who are My Guides?

White Feather, my main guide, is a beautiful, large being and my gatekeeper with my mediumship. Often, our main guide is a soul we have had a past life with. This guide is highly compassionate, gentle, loving and caring, and helps protect our soul, aura and chakras from unnecessary and inappropriate energies when we're consciously doing light work. Once we pass into the spirit world, we're joined by our main guide and our soul group—others of our own vibration—after we have had our life revision or review of how well we did on Earth with all our spiritual contracts.

As a working medium, my own gatekeeper was introduced to me a long time ago, before I knew I would be working full-time as a medium and it would become my life's work. While I was meditating one day, a gentle voice asked me to draw a picture of a Native American with great white feathers on his head. This was not an ordinary man, but a great chief. When I asked what the connection was, my higher self—my own soul energy within—told me I was once this great chief's son, and we had a very loving and connected life together. He called himself White Feather, or Father.

Not long after meeting him, I was shown, in dreams, images of our life together in an Indigenous community gathering, next to a river, with horses and campfires, somewhere in America. Suddenly, tears filled my eyes because the love I felt was overwhelming, and it stayed with me for days. The love continued and was indescribable. I felt I was truly connected to the source of Great Spirit.

Romanov: Romanov and White Feather seem to work together a lot, especially during my private séances. I would describe this guide as a large spirit man, who has a beard and wears a turban. When I tuned into a trance state, I was told that while on Earth, Romanov had lived in the time of Ancient Egypt, when he worked as a mystic. This spirit entity also appeared in the $15^{th} - 18^{th}$ centuries.

I believe Romanov is a wise spiritual teacher. He shows me how to be strong, and how to be more discerning with people, instead of just rushing in before I really know who I'm dealing with. Too often, I've befriended people who have really had no interest in me at all except what I could do for them.

This powerful and clever guide assists me in my personal readings and club shows by helping me line up the spirit people who want to come through with the spirit communicators' messages, as well as gathering survival evidence, when I connect to loved ones in spirit.

It works like this. As I am clairaudient, I listen, hear a name and call it out to the audience. Then, once I've connected to the client, I listen again and receive messages that only the client will know about. In many cases, I feel a pulling sensation when I find the right person in the audience, and sometimes I actually see a spirit person standing next to that person.

Dr Lee: As mentioned earlier, Dr Lee is a healing Reiki guide who first appeared when I studied Reiki and became a master in my early days. He works with energy and meridians within the body. He is quite serious, dedicated and very bossy. He is a Japanese gentleman, with tiny hands and wears his hair in a long plait. He has a restless nature, similar to my own, and is a curious, intelligent being who likes to get on with the job at hand.

There was a time when I did a lot of healing work and psychic surgery in a trance state. This phase soon passed as I went in a different direction, but when I began working with his energy, I found myself attracting numerous clients who possibly had cancer or other serious problems within their bodies. I also started doing psychic surgery with my healings. I had no idea what I was doing and simply surrendered to the energy and acted as a pure channel for the work that needed to be done.

Spiritual psychic surgery is a non-invasive event involving the physical body. It operates by drawing negative energy out of the energy body or field, removing deep-rooted blocks of stagnant and negative energy from the body and energy centres or chakras. It also removes thought forms and memory implants, or what we call 'soul retrieval'. If not removed, these energies can create disease, leading to strangulation of the organs and body parts on an emotional and physical level, blocking the life force and possibly leading to long-term health problems.

This type of hands-on healing is completely different to the psychic surgery, prominent in the 1960s – 1980s, practised in the Philippines and other areas in the world where tumours and other diseased tissue are removed from inside the body.

Reiki energy and other methods of spiritual healing work effectively alongside conventional healing and can accelerate the healing process. I should emphasise that I would never suggest to a client to go off their medication unless their doctor told them to do so.

Over the years, I also learnt to create many powerful crystal layouts – using grids and placing the stones on the body's energy centres– since crystals are excellent conduits and amplifiers of energy. While I have cut back on my hands-on healing work, I mostly do remote healing now, as it is easy and just as effective.

Animals also love spiritual energy, as do plants. I love to do remote healing for the planet as well, including forests, rivers, and other waterways. Nature is so good for all of us; it is very healing for the soul, mind, body and spirit.

Throughout a mediumship, guides will come and go. For example, I worked with Dr Lee, my Reiki guide, for many years. When I stopped working with clients, he stepped back so other guides could work with me instead, depending on the work I was doing.

Margaret: Margaret is an older wise woman guide who once worked as a clairvoyant, white witch and healer in England. When I connect to her energy through a light trance, she speaks with a distinct English accent. She works with flower essences and mediumship. She has also taught me how to remove entities from auras; how to undertake spirit rescue (removing lost souls from houses); and how to get rid of spells and curses.

Margaret lived during the 18th century and did not like the church, as it condemned her work, despite being someone who helped heal people or contact their loved ones on the other side. I've had the most amazing insights by working with this very kind and humble guide, who constantly teaches me things I couldn't possibly know or have read in a book.

I have worked with Margaret on many spirit rescues, which is when a person doesn't pass over to the other side and becomes what we call 'earthbound'. These people are often unaware they are dead, and in some cases are very scared or may not know where they are. This can happen if, for example, they have been in an accident and experienced sudden death, or even if they have behaved badly and think they're going to end up in hell, which is a make-believe place by the way.

With my guide Margaret, I'm also able to remove what we call entities, which are lower vibrational parasites, from the aura. We sometimes pick up these energies when the outer layer of our aura becomes thin and breaks or rips. This can happen through drug use, shock, long-term sickness, trauma, alcoholism, accidents, stress, and so on. Once I've scanned an aura with my hands and third eye, I'm able to send these pests into the light for healing. I'm also able to remove curses that may have been around for centuries and may be very harmful to people.

Most people know when they have been cursed, as nothing works in their lives, no matter how hard they try, and they go around and around, never getting anywhere. Often their love life is a shambles as well. These people usually know something is wrong, but don't know what to do about it. The lucky ones will be guided by their loving spirit guides to reputable healers who work in this area and can help them.

I always feel safe when Margaret is around as she is very competent and knows exactly what she is doing.

Cassandra: Cassandra is a beautiful, kind and gentle angel whose main goal is to help as many people as possible. She talks about and teaches me the importance of love, forgiveness and kindness. She has a special yearning to help children, animals, and all humankind. The first time I channelled this being, I felt very honoured. This delightful light being has not only graced me with her presence, but has also taught me, on so many levels, how important it is to honour and love myself as an eternal soul.

Never feel, for one minute, less than others around you. When you learn this simple lesson, people will respect you more because this is the energy you ultimately give out. What you believe you become.

Cassandra also talks about taking time out to nurture ourselves, something many of us find hard to achieve, as we are so busy.

Leon: This guide is quite a character and one of my favourite enlightened beings in the team of spiritual guides I work with. He has a similar personality to mine: he is a practical joker and likes to see the funny side of things. Seriously, too much gloom and doom is not a good thing, and only drags you down to places that you really don't want to go to.

Leon is what I call my 'writer guide' and has helped me with the many books I've written. It's as if I hear direction from an unknown source. The first time I channelled Leon, I couldn't wipe the smile off my face because he was so pretentious and snobby. This amusing and creative guide has been part of my life for as far back as I can remember.

I've always been driven to express myself artistically, including wanting to be an actor. Creative writing was my favourite subject at school because it gave me time to daydream. Music is also very good for artistic expression, and I played in many bands as a bass player when I was younger.

Around the same time Leon came through, I visited a psychic artist. I laughed, stunned, when I saw what the artist had drawn. It was Leon. He looked like a very old hippy from the late 1950s or early 1960s, complete with a cigarette hanging from his mouth.

Leon is an artist in every sense of the word. When he talks, he's loud and bombastic to the point of hysterics, waves his hands around, and talks with a plum in his mouth, something I would never do.

Erin: Tiny Erin is a mischievous nature fairy, or undine, who likes to travel around on the back of birds. I have enjoyed channelling her over the years because whenever she comes through, the room fills with mirth and gaiety. This wise being helps me appreciate nature, and I always feel her presence when I'm in our garden or making flower essences for clients or walking in the bush.

When I channel this sprite, I'm full of giggles and feel like a child again. Her personality is utterly charming, innocent and sweet.

I also feel she helps me with my inner child, by teaching me to play and not take life so seriously.

Whenever I'm clearing my yard or making major changes in the garden, such as renovations or tree or shrub removal, I always say a little prayer or ask the nature spirits for permission before I go ahead. I've noticed people who haven't done this, have later had major problems with water and electricity. Whenever this happens, I always put it down to a disgruntled sprite.

I have a lovely fairy garden in the front of my yard, hidden amongst the trees and bushes, where I place my sick plants for the nature spirits to heal. They always end up becoming healthier and happier than ever before.

Red Hawk: Red Hawk is a gentle energy and guide who works with my mediumship, helping spirit people cross over through spirit rescue. To me, he looks like a young Native American with long dark hair and simple clothes. He stays very much in the background, saying little, but is happy to assist when needed. He's very humble, and I feel as though I've been a brother to him in a past life as a Native American.

Every time I channel Red Hawk in trance, I feel like I'm riding a horse bareback on a great open prairie. He always comes with strong messages of reassurance that in death, we are never alone on our journey to the other side.

Johnny: Johnny is a young spirit boy who died in a children's hospital at the age of eight. He first introduced himself to the séance group a couple of years later, when I was raising money for kids with cancer. He said he and some other spirit children wanted to work with my group and help with the spirit phenomenon that was always occurring during our séances.

While the group was running, Johnny and four other spirit children stayed with us until I closed the group. In hindsight, I can see that we, as a group, were fortunate to work with so many beautiful spirit children over the years, as we received so much joy and laughter while working together. We organised a small tree at Christmas, with five Christmas balls, one for each spirit child, in appreciation, love and gratitude for these children's invaluable service over the years. In the weeks that followed, we sang Christmas songs.

4
MEET MY STAR SEED GUIDES

For millennia, ancient civilisations have looked to the skies, connecting to the planets and other galaxies, to receive wisdom, insight and information far greater than themselves. Some people have reported strange alien abductions or interventions leaving them confused, such as being taken aboard advanced ships and travelling rapidly to distant galaxies. Whether in their dreams or in an altered state, this is evidence we live in an incredible, multifaceted universe of many possibilities.

When you think about it, why is it not possible to have intergalactic friends who could maybe teach us a thing or two? These beings could have been observing Earth for years and keeping an eye on what's going on: we are seeing more and more sightings, which is interesting.

I have always believed that every element in our bodies was once a star. I have come to learn, and am amazed by the fact, there are so many brilliant and sensitive beings all over the world who are drawn to the stars and may even have lived past lives on different planets, in other galaxies and dimensions.

It is my belief that highly advanced and intelligent children are born every day. These amazing souls are called hybrid souls because they carry the DNA strands of both human and galactic beings, and their purpose is to share their unique abilities by helping humanity, while embracing their Earth experience. Through my research, past-life regression work, and private sittings, I have discovered these hybrid souls have lived mostly on peaceful planets as extraterrestrial beings, from physical or non-physical galaxies. It's my understanding, from a spiritual perspective, they are here to support their own ascension and to help others awaken through their spiritual growth and earthly journey. One could also say perhaps they're here for the good of the planet, to serve humanity and bring more light and a higher consciousness to the planet, helping in our own evolution.

Star Seed Guides I have Channelled

As a teenager, when surfing and camping with my friends, I was always staring at the stars, the moon and the planet Venus, wondering if people from other worlds really lived in these places. This has always been a source of fascination and deep curiosity for me. It was always something my friends and I discussed, for as far back as I can remember.

I've seen unusual lights in the northern sky and have been convinced these are craft, and I know many people have had similar experiences, which are not to be ignored.

As a trance channel, physical medium and natural medium, I work with various guides in both my trance work and closed-group séances, including star beings. I know have had past lives on other planets and have a hybrid soul. I believe that many like me live on Earth to support humanity's growth amid planetary and energetic changes.

Recently, I've met others who also feel they've lived on other planets; together, we aim to help raise awareness across fields such as the environment, social media, spirituality, the arts, science, and medicine.

As a trance medium, I'm able to channel interesting light beings for my own development to help people. For example, over the years, I've channelled healing symbols to help with illnesses. All types of healing have always interested me, starting with my early nursing days, working in Australia and overseas as a registered nurse.

I work with many guides across different aspects of my work, but I have three star-being guides who have been with me for many years. They constantly give me information and teach me about healing through my trance work. Through this, I'm able to send healing energy to the world in meditation and to my clients, loved ones and the groups I work with.

The three very humble star-being guides continue to keep me fascinated on this continual journey of learning. I also have a passion for the Pleiades system (an open star cluster containing over 1,000 stars, though only about six to seven are visible to the naked eye, earning it the name 'Seven Sisters'), and I have met people in my life who say they have guides from there as well.

These three guides are Dr Lennox, from the Andromeda system; Three of One, from the Arcturus system; and Zeek from the Zeta race.

Dr Lennox: Dr Lennox is a tall star being from the Andromeda system. He first started coming through in my private séances. He's a healing guide and will often share information about illnesses in the body, offering healing to us all. He's quite remarkable. One woman who sat in the group said she was thrilled when he worked energetically on her eyesight, which improved after a couple of sessions.

In the séance, Dr Lennox told the group, through me, that he had lived on Earth in an early century as a doctor. Generous to the core, he's also quite humorous, and when I run workshops, he likes to help people with their ailments, and will give suggestions on health, diet and general wellbeing, so long as it's in accordance with their own doctors.

Often when he comes through, the sitters will all say what an unusual character he is and how funny he is. They say he is often with other beings in the room, who are tall, blue, and seem to stand at the back of the group. When this occurs, a buzzing sound can be heard, the temperature in the room will become warmer, and, to the delight of the sitters, they will often see a fantastic light show, which is described as a peek into the galaxy—truly unforgettable, to say the least.

Three of One: Three of One is a delightful and highly intelligent star being. He was the first star being to come through, and is an unusually tall character consisting of sheer pure light, with a long neck that feels difficult when I channel him. I was later told he's an Arcturian from the Arcturus star system, and he is a blue colour. Edgar Cayce, the world-renowned psychic and healer, said in his teachings Arcturus is one of the most advanced civilizations in this galaxy. It is the fifth-dimensional civilisation that is a prototype of Earth's future. Its energy works as an emotional, mental and spiritual healer for humanity. It's also an energy gateway through which humans pass during death and rebirth. It functions as a waystation for non-physical consciousness to become accustomed to physicality.

Unfortunately, Three of One's own planet in the Arcturus system was destroyed long ago, so he lives on spaceships with other light beings, all of which communicate telepathically with one another through soundwaves. Like other beings from other planets, here on Earth, he is helping humankind with the changes we are experiencing on our planet. There are many beings and hybrids like Three of One here today, helping and working with the ascension and growth of our sacred planet, mother Earth.

Three of One's interests include teleportation, healing with symbols, and teaching people to become empowered and more aware of their own abilities. He has given me a few symbols for different uses, which I use with all my healing work. These symbols are not cures, but simply ways to attract the right energy for the healing, that client may need in conjunction with any other conventional therapies they may be using.

Sitters have told me Three of One usually arrives in the next room in a spaceship with flashing lights. When they see the coloured lights through the glass door, they know he has arrived.

Zeek: Zeek is a friendly, small grey being I have begun going into trance with, during my closed-séance groups. I find it amazing how many people think the grey extra-terrestrials (ETs) are dangerous. I have only ever worked with benevolent souls, so nothing bad has ever come into the séance energy. My spirit team is very protective of me, so this would never happen anyway. The small beings are not unsafe and simply work as observers of the world. As an aside, I have heard from others that it's the tall ones we need to be wary of.

Zeek, who claims to be from the Zeta race, has visited my séance group before. I've known other mediums who work with these sentient beings a lot and experience the wonderous healing they assist with.

Zeek is of small stature, with a big head, and speaks through me, the channel. The sitters find his manner matter-of-fact. Others have told me the greys are emotionless, intelligent and telepathic, but I feel this particular being is the total opposite, and very compassionate.

Before Zeek and the other star beings came into the closed group, the sitters would often witness a flashing light show, with some type of rounded, small disc shaped spaceship, also emitting flashing lights. After a few minutes, the spaceship would disappear. The beings would take time to speak and introduce themselves.

Zeek, often talked about world politics and healing when the sitters asked questions, as they were very curious to hear what he had to say. He would always say he was an observer only and wouldn't consider telling us what to do.

After channelling him in a trance state, I would be extremely tired for a few days afterwards, as I wasn't used to the energy it took to channel this star being. Other mediums and psychics I've spoken to have claimed the same, and one man in particular told me, at one stage he couldn't get out of bed for a week. Whether I choose to continue to work with this being in the future is debatable, considering the energy it takes. The Arcturian and Andromeda energy is easier for my body to channel.

Healing Symbols I have Received

I've always had a fascination with symbols, which isn't surprising as I'm a Reiki Master and a Seichim Master. I've always had an openness and love for the idea of using ancient symbols for healing, as they are so effortless to use and work incredibly effectively.

I've discovered over the years these symbols are easy to use in séances. Draw them in through the crown chakra energy centre, which sits at the top of the head and make a *whooshing* sound when doing so. You only need to place the symbols in once but always follow your own intuition.

When you have the need to do so, you can also draw them on the palms of your hands, where your hand chakras are. As you draw the symbol, you need to make the whooshing sound with each line you draw. When you make a symbol, the sound is very important, as it seals the energy and the healing will be more effective. For example: *whoosh, whoosh, whoosh.* Once you've done this, place your hands on the top of your head on the crown chakra.

You can also use them on animals, birds and plants, anything that is living, as we are all energy.

The Cancer Symbol

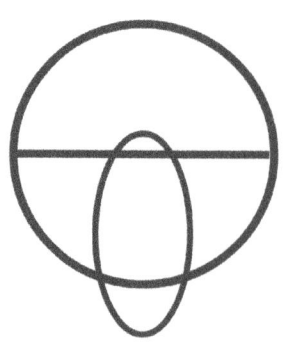

The cancer symbol first came to me in a séance I was running with my private group. My guide, Three of One, came in at the end of the session and showed it to me. I couldn't believe what was happening, because, at the time, my father was going to have an operation for cancer of the brain, caused by a squamous cell carcinoma, due to spending many hours in the sun in his job as a waterside worker.

After the 15-hour operation, my mother rang me. I went straight to the ICU, placed the healing symbol in my father's crown chakra and poured energy in. After I was finished, I prayed for healing and his recovery. He has been in remission for eight years now, and he has had a wonderful life, apart from the fact that he lost half of his face and an eye, after his surgery.

I believe the cancer symbol helped my father because it was not his time karmically; the healing with the symbol was accepted for his highest good. We were so grateful for this miracle, and to have him stay longer in our family. My brother has his own set of challenges, and Mum often said she needed Dad's support for as long as possible.

The Arthritis Symbol

I like to draw the arthritis symbol on the palms of my hands and place energy directly on the area, for example, my knee. With weights and exercise, I have used this technique to great effect and have very little trouble now. I use the symbol only when I need it.

The Clearing, or Detox, Symbol

The clearing or detox symbol can be used with any illness, or when intuitively needed. It's very good for all children and seems to help children with additional needs as well. I like to place this on my crown chakra once a week if I'm unwell, or until I feel better. In conjunction with other modalities, it's a safe and positive symbol to use.

5
SÉANCES AND MEDIUMSHIP

The word séance comes from the French word *session*. It first became a thing in the second half of the 19th century, when groups of spiritualists and mediums began advocating the use of specialised tools during séances to communicate with loved ones in spirit and other spirit people. A séance is led by the allocated medium, who goes into a light or deep trance state and channels the visiting spirit's energy and messages.

Probably the most renowned figures in the history of séances, are the three Fox sisters from Rochester. Celebrity mediums in 19th century New York, they played a pivotal role in shaping the birth of the modern Spiritualism movement.

What is Physical Mediumship?

Physical mediumship is understood as the manipulation of energies and energy systems by spirits and includes a wide range of phenomena. This type of mediumship is said to involve perceptible manifestations, such as loud raps, materialised voices, apports, or the appearance of spirit bodies or partial forms such as hands, legs and feet.

Through extensive training and practice, and many long hours of sittings, mediums learn to attune to different frequencies. This allows the spirit world to work with the medium during demonstrations of either mental or physical mediumship.

The primary purpose of all mediumships is to provide proof of the immortality of human existence. The catalyst for all physical mediumship is the level of spiritual atonement, or reactiveness, we hold toward the spirit person we are communicating with. This state is called trance mediumship, which takes many years of study and dedication to master.

What is Trance Mediumship?

Trance mediumship is a deeper aspect of mediumship which influences your work and spirituality. It is the ability to blend your energies with the spirit control and the medium. It occurs when your conscious mind is subdued, slowing down your thoughts so the spirits may impress their presence on your mind. In this state, you can be in touch with, and at one with minds which influence, educate, uplift, and inspire.

To achieve this state of trance, you must withdraw your awareness from the here and now and move your mind into that aspect of stillness. As you do this, the spirit world will move closer to you, as the medium, until there is very little awareness or consciousness.

Trance mediumship involves a special relationship with the guides who work with you. This helps build rapport and may bring a sharper, more specific and more accurate flow of information across all areas of healing, mediumship, philosophy, and teaching. This is the best way to learn who you are working with in your own spirit team, as they are the spiritual teachers who will constantly help and educate you along the way.

What is Transfiguration Mediumship?

A transfiguration medium can communicate, like other mediums, with those in the spirit world. It's about blending vibrations and energy with the spirit in question to forge the connection. In my private séances, the sitters will often say when I bring spirits through in deep trance, they see other people's images on my face, those I may be connecting to at the time. Once the message has been delivered, my face will return to normal again. When you develop sufficiently to achieve the trance state, it means you've gotten out of your own way of thinking and blended with the spirit energy.

Physical Mediumship and Séances

The first séance I ever attended was led by a trained medium from the local spiritualist church I had attended for many years. As sitters, we were told each of us would have a turn at being the main channel, working with our spirit team in trance. Normally, we would have sat in a darkened room in a large cabinet structure, but on this occasion, we sat on chairs away from the others.

The group – a circle of eight people – directed energy to the medium, whose turn it was to go into trance, create the phenomena, and bring through messages from the guide or spirit people. As our teacher went under, it was easy to see the spirit overshadow her, a process called transfiguration. She was a very good teacher, and we were all encouraged to have a go.

At first, I was fearful. Since childhood I had been terrified of the dark, often attracting all types of spirit traffic as soon as the lights went out. Yet, as spirit teaches, our lives are preordained through spiritual contracts made before we're born. And before long, I was learning much about the spirit world I hadn't known.

Living only five minutes from that church, walking there was easy … for my cats. I arrived one day to find one of my cats sitting comfortably in a chair at the side of the circle, waiting patiently for me. All my cats had sat in on my trance and meditation classes for years or hung around outside the doors to my small office where I held classes, so, although amusing, it was no real surprise to see him there. Still, it gave me great comfort, and when I called his name, he pretended to ignore me, making the other sitters and mediums laugh and breaking the ice.

After about a year, feeling confident with the training from my teacher at the time, White Feather appeared in meditation and suggested it was time to move on. I was told not to worry about anything – my spirit team and guides would support me. All I needed was to sit with people more like myself and remember to have a good time; things did not have to be as serious as the circles I had been part of up to now.

Soon after, I began receiving many spirit signs, such as seeing white feathers everywhere. I'm happy to say it wasn't long before I had a full circle of main sitters who stayed with me for many years, in fact until the day I eventually closed the group.

6
RUNNING MY OWN HOME CIRCLE

Within weeks, I was running my own group, going into the trance state, and everything started to move as it should. I was now ready to progress with the work and was very grateful to have a room full of devoted and supportive sitters who loved every minute of the whole exciting experience.

White Feather's guidance led me to feel more confident since I was with like-minded people, and I had no spirits prodding me in the back, trying to get my attention all the time, because I was the one going under into trance. I felt proud and honoured to be working with my dear friends, my beloved spirit team. And the good thing about running my own séances was that I was no longer scared of the dark.

Jimmy, my main sitter or control, was an ex-drummer I had known for many years. Jimmy controlled the group when I went under, and we were joined by the most beautiful, dedicated and loving sitters, which always made each occasion a wonderful and fun time.

When I first opened my small séance group in the office at the back of my house, it really took off and we had some amazing nights. Eventually, after a few years, I had to move it away from my home. The energy was huge, and my husband began complaining when a few of the spirit visitors decided they wanted to stay, even though I had closed down the group, and move into our home. My daughters would also complain about seeing spirits walking around. They weren't scared, just annoyed, and found it invasive.

After upending my whole family's living arrangements—with things being moved around, lights going on and off, and upsetting the cats, which were hysterical by this stage—my husband said he had no idea what I was up to, but it was enough.

I moved the group up the road to my office, where I saw clients in my healing and reading practice. It didn't take long until the group energy built up again, and we were joined by Johnny and the spirit children, Romanov and the rest of my spirit team. This was remarkable, to say the least.

All the sitters loved Johnny and used to squeal with delight at his funny antics. Every time he worked with us, he always had something to say and had the sitters in stitches while he led the other spirit children who came in to assist. Without a doubt, he was the leader of the children, and he guided them in pushing the small table around and around, while bringing in visiting spirits who wanted to come through and talk on the night.

One of the sitters said she often felt Johnny next to her in the car on the way home after the sessions, which brought her comfort and made her feel safe. Another surprising thing was when Johnny came through, he often seemed to know what was going on in our private lives. We soon learnt there were no secrets, which also made us laugh.

We had many experiences of this over the years. One time Johnny told us all, in a cheeky way, about one of the sitters and her new boyfriend. Another time, one of the sitters experienced a spiritual phenomenon when she had a ring taken off her finger and placed on her other hand—even though I had consistently told sitters not to wear jewellery.

The Benefits of Working as a Psychical Medium

One thing I have discovered over the years is working directly with spirit has opened me up in the areas of clairvoyance (clear seeing), clairsentience (clear feeling, or 'gut feelings'), clairaudience (clear hearing) and clairalience (clear smelling). In fact, all my mediumship qualities have vastly improved in every way. One downside is I now have an oversensitive nose, although I also use my sense of smell when doing spirit rescue.

White Feather has shown me images of the spirit world while I'm in a deep trance state, but what we see depends on what the guides want to show us and based on the ongoing dialogue within the group.

Over the years, I've sat with some wonderful physical mediums, with excellent training, who were far more advanced than me. One remarkable man I took a workshop with, a visiting German medium, was very encouraging. He told me with a laugh that I had a whole entourage of English spirits, or guides, working with me in my spirit team. From that day on, I never looked back, as he gave me the information I needed to know to keep doing my work. His kind message provided the encouragement I needed to continue, at a time when I was feeling unsupported by other physical mediums in the industry.

Wanting as much information as I could, I researched the work of Robin Foy, an English physical medium, an expert in his field, who had experienced many years of séance phenomena and dramatic communications with famous and ordinary people. I was especially interested in his pioneering role with the Scole Experimental Group, he ran years ago, and his contact with the spirit of Winston Churchill. When I read of the remarkable work he had accomplished, I saw this as a sign that anything is possible. Inspired and excited, I chose to shape my own circle as an experimental closed group as well, with the same sitters, who, after many years, still sit with me today.

This group took on a life of its own, bringing messages from not only the sitters' relatives, but also from famous people who chose to drop in from the worlds of music, the arts and sport. Interestingly, I never requested anyone to drop in. I always left this up to the spirit control and Johnny.

7
CONDUCTING SÉANCES: A COMPLETE GUIDE

If you have an interest in physical mediumship and séances, you'll be shown another world, but first, you need to do a bit of research, so you have an understanding of what goes on. The first thing is to watch someone, as a sitter, who does this work and has a good reputation in the industry.

Getting Started with Séance Work

Not everyone will have success, no matter how much time they put into the training, and most often it's because of their spirit team. This work is not for the novice.

If you feel that you have what it takes, when you're in the flow and feel a calling, take the time to look for an established group that offers training in physical mediumship. Remember, with all types of spiritual mediumship, you need to have the right spirit team who wants to work with you and progress you through the many levels. For example, I'm able to do spirit-rescue work as part of my practice because I have the right spirit team to support me. Not every medium can do this.

You need to sit in a group with a trained medium who has a good reputation, is trained in trance work and knows exactly what they're doing. Ideally, they should have years of experience and also work with a person who acts as a control. The control is the person who runs the group throughout the session and helps bring the spirits through by introducing them to the group. For example, the control might say: 'I'd like to ask the medium if there's anybody who wants to come through tonight.'

Physical mediumship is rare. It takes years of dedication, with regular sittings and devoted, good people. It's something you cannot rush, as this aspect of mediumship is run by the spirit world. If your spirit team doesn't want you to sit, the group will be closed down, or you will have poor results, which will seem like a waste of time.

Preparing for a Séance: What to Wear and Bring

I recommend that you wear comfortable dark clothes, rather than light or bright clothing. No jewellery is allowed. Items such as watches, necklaces or hairclips, can be moved around by the spirits during the séance. One sitter, who didn't listen to my rules, had a spirit try to rip out one of her earrings. Going by her screams, I'm sure it was very painful.

In my private séances, I always asked for phones to be turned off, and for people to wear dark clothes, no jewellery, nothing in their hair, and to keep any problems they were having in their private lives outside the room. It was a sacred space, and negative energy was not welcome on the night. I would also ask sitters not to talk about what went on, as the séances were private and not for sharing with the general public.

Setting Up the Séance Room

The séance room is always darkened. Some mediums will use a cabinet, which can be used like a very small room, or sit in a chair away from the group. There is usually a small table as well, placed between the medium and the sitters, which can spin when moved by the spirit children.

Once everyone was sitting comfortably in their regular seats, the room was completely blacked out; there was no light at all, except a red light in the background to enhance spirit activity. (When working with trance mediumship, a blue light is used.)

The sitters formed a small circle around the table, which was in the middle of the room and had a trumpet on top. When required, the sitters placed their hands on the table until it spun around by itself, with the help of the spirit children. We also have a traditional array of tools and appurtenances, including a spirit trumpet, a small levitation table and other toys that are used by the spirits.

Using Red and Blue Lights

I like to use coloured lights in my séance work, as they serve important purposes in creating the right conditions for spirit phenomena.

Red Light

Using a red light in the darkened séance room enables the sitter to see the transfiguration of the person (physical medium) before them. Spirit will often produce a mask over the face of the medium to form a likeness of themselves, which is usually formed from ectoplasm, a light-coloured, viscous substance built up by the medium. Normally it's only visible in the darkened atmosphere of a séance. Facial features and hair can also be changed, as in transfiguration. The colour red is also a conduit to attract more physical energy into the room.

Blue Light

Blue light is always used in trance sessions, as it quiets and slows the energy and spirit activity. It's associated with a sense of peace, intuition and connection to higher realms. It's often used to signify spirit presence, or as a symbolic representation of calmness during sessions.

Rules and Respect for Sacred Space

The séance is held at a designated time, and once the group is open and the process has begun, the doors are closed. Latecomers are not welcome because they would break the energy the medium and the sitters have built up once the séance has started.

There's no room for any type of mind-altering drugs or alcohol in my groups, and the sitters need to respect this. I never allow anyone who is a heavy substance abuser in, as it's my preference for the energy to be clean. I once had to turn down a potential sitter who asked to sit in with my group because I knew she was a daily pot smoker, something I will not tolerate.

Séances are not silly games for ignorant people looking for a laugh; they are to be treated with respect. It's a beautiful way of connecting to, and receiving, heartfelt messages from loved ones in the spirit world. It is also a beautiful way of receiving healing from the spirit world, as the spirit goes to great lengths to make the connection. Everyone needs to be openminded. They must be aware of sending good energy to the medium and stay focused to help create the energy and links for the medium to build up in the room.

As spirit generally controls the outcome of the group energy, anyone who is not compatible with the energies will usually be moved on by the medium's spirit team in very subtle ways and will not return to the circle. When people leave, they are energetically cut off from the group's oversoul by the medium, making it impossible for them to tune in to what's going on at the next meeting. Sitters need to be aware of and respect any rules set by the medium and the control running the group.

Protection: Opening and Closing Prayers

The medium may also choose to have their hands tied and agree to be searched prior to the session, to ensure they have no tokens or objects on their body to throw into the middle of the room, which is fraudulent.

It's my firm belief when doing any type of spiritual work, it's important to set up protection before you start, and to have the sitters close down their energy centres, or chakras, afterwards. This is done by the control, who offers a prayer while opening the group at the beginning of the session and again when closing. When the night is over, and the medium is ready to come back into the room, the energy is closed down again with a prayer, and any lingering spirits are asked to leave and go into the light.

The opening prayer usually starts like this: 'Great Spirit, we ask to work in the light. Let love and light be our guides. We ask to work in the light always and ask for protection always.'

The closing prayer may go like this: 'Great Spirit, thank you for your assistance tonight and for working with us in the light. We appreciate your loving guidance, protection and light. We ask that any lingering spirits return to where they come from. Until next time. Thank you.'

Working with Spirit and Group Energy

During a séance, we work only with loving higher entities, and loved ones who come with messages of love, information and healing. We don't talk to lower entities in the astral which haven't crossed over to the spirit world, who are troublesome and looking for mischief. Who we sit with is also important. This is because everyone is blending their energies and working together as one, assisting with the energy for the medium, who is in a trance state. The group is also working with their own spirit guides, as well as the medium's spirit team.

The Séance Process: Step by Step

Once the sitters are ready, the control, or main sitter, opens with a prayer of protection. From this point on, the control person runs the group, asking who the medium is with and ensuring no one leaves their seats until the medium is back in their body. Then the group is closed down. There is only one person who goes into a trance state to lead the group, and that is the designated medium.

Some people, however, don't like rules. I once had a student who, unbeknownst to me, decided to go into trance as well, and started bringing messages through on his own, without my or the group's permission. I had to close down the group immediately, with the help of my main control. Once I was back in my body, we kicked the offending person out and told him never to return as he obviously had no respect for the rules.

The group would open with a protective prayer and a blessing by the main sitter, or control. The control's role in the séance group was to open and close the group, keep a protective eye on the medium, organise the songs, turn the music on and off, and, as each spirit came through, ask Johnny, the spirit communicator, who I was speaking with.

Then, after the opening prayer, I would give an address, in the trance state, from my spirit team. Once the address was finished, we play uplifting music while all the sitters sing along. Singing songs and playing music lifts the energy in the room and encourages loved ones and spirits to come and join us.

After the sitters had finished singing, Jimmy, the control, would always ask if any spirits wanted to come through me and speak.

Once a few spirit people had come through, usually two to begin with, I was able to go deeper into the trance state. This intensified the energy from the spirit world, which created different types of spiritual phenomena, such as flashing lights, orbs, spirit faces in the trumpet, and the sound of rapping on the walls. Often, the table would jump or spin around madly, and at times it even seemed to leap high in the air.

Types of Phenomena You May Experience

Types of phenomena can include knocking on walls, being touched by spirits, the appearance of spirit voices, tables spinning and rocking without help, cones being lifted, bells ringing, lights flashing, orbs, and the sensation of cold or hot air. A séance can also include spirits and spirit children walking and running around the room, created by ectoplasm taken from the cells of the medium and sometimes the séance attendees. There may also be transfigurations of different spirits over the medium. When this happens, it's of course very moving for all the sitters.

At this point in a session, the sitters would be very excited, yelling they could see spirit people walking around the room and spirit children running wildly around the table. Some sitters would say they could also feel invisible fingers on their back, or some of the spirit people touching them on the head. Towards the end of my experimental days, spiritual apports would sometimes, but not often, drop from the ether into the room—these instances were gifts from the spirit world.

Once, during a session, a large rock was teleported from the room next door through the wall into our séance room, where it dropped to the floor. More advanced psychical mediums, than me, have had many apports, such as coins, crystals, feathers, flowers or small tokens. I once received a small cross in a sitting I attended, and one gifted psychical medium I know can have crystals come through his mouth.

Going further into the sessions, we would experience more phenomena. The temperature of the room would change, either becoming freezing cold, warming up or the sitters would sometimes feel warm or cold breezes. The table would sometimes keep spinning around in time to the music, as if it had a life of its own. More spirit people would come in and speak through me. When this happened, Jimmy, the control, would turn the music off and ask if anyone else wanted to come through me and speak. This process would be repeated a few times during the session.

Sometimes sitters shared they had experienced hundreds of white orbs on the floor and in the air, which floated around and moved objects, such as the toys we placed in the room for spirits to play with. Some toys were fluorescent and could be seen in the dark, while others were squeaky toys that made a sound when touched by the spirit people. And sometimes there were pleasant smells of flowers or perfume.

With more experienced physical mediums, materialised bodies, including heads, hands or feet, and spirit people can be seen walking around the room. And in some instances, the medium uses other people's energy to help with their own connection to the spirit world. I personally have never used human batteries, unlike some mediums I've sat with do.

Spirit Healing During Séances

I've also worked with spirit doctors who offer healing for the group. One woman said she asked for healing for her eyes and phoned me a week later to say there'd been some improvement, according to her specialist. I doubt if she told them of her involvement in my group.

Additionally, when spirit doctors have visited, the guides and spirit team will always advise using white sheets on the person's bed if they want healing, like in a hospital, and to call them in so they can continue working on them while they sleep. Spirit doctors have also told sitters to call them in whenever their assistance is needed. Many of my sitters have phoned me after these sessions, to let me know how things have gone, and they will often report their illness or disease has improved, or that certain parts of their bodies have been healed.

Towards the end of a night (after about an hour and a half), the energy would suddenly drop and everything would slow down. This was the signal to call in the healing guides for spirit doctors, for the group healing time. Once this was completed, Johnny, the spirit communicator, would announce the session was coming to an end.

At the end, we also discussed the healing session and asked if anyone had experienced any healing from the spirit doctors.

Closing the Séance

Then Jimmy, the control, would say goodbye to everyone, thank the spirit children for their help and close down the session with a prayer, which would go like this:

> *Thank you, Johnny and the spirit children, for working with us tonight. Thank you also for all the wonderful words of wisdom from the spirits that came through the medium tonight. Again, we thank Great Spirit for another wonderful night of communication and healing. We now ask for any unwanted spirits or lost spirits to go into the light as well.*

The Lord's Prayer would follow this. Then I would be called back into the room. After a few minutes, I was back in my body again, able to listen to others and chat about the night's occurrences, including who had come in, what we had learnt, and what type of phenomena we had experienced.

Then we would all have a light supper and go home.

My Personal Experience with Séances

My private sittings with a group of good friends were always joyous, wonderful occasions, like parties, and something in my life I will never forget. There was always lots of laughter, singing and fun entertainment. It always made me smile when I went under as the trance medium in those group sessions, as I would never know who was going to come through. The good thing was that I always felt safe, and it was always an honour.

Whenever I was in the trance state, I could still hear what was going on around me.

When I did this work with my spirit team, I did not want to go too deep into the trance state and remember nothing afterwards, but some nights I did go very deep and had to rely on the sitters to tell me what happened later.

During the sessions, as I sat back from the group, I was amused to hear them laughing, singing and carrying on. No matter how loud it got, I was still able to concentrate on what I was doing. When I brought the spirits in and channelled their energy and messages, the room became silent as the sitters listened and then asked questions of the spirit person who was talking through me.

Famous Spirits Coming Through

Over time, Johnny, our main spirit communicator, not only brought in loved ones and pets through me, but also famous icons and celebrities we all knew and loved from yesteryear. They had all been popular and loved in their day.

At first, we were all starstruck and surprised, and eventually delighted. We couldn't believe what was happening, but we just went with it. It was so exciting, and all the sitters had so many questions, as you can imagine. If nothing else, it was a change in direction from where we had been and where we were heading. The best thing was, we never knew beforehand who would be arriving on any given night.

The first famous spirit to come into the séance was John Lennon, who I had written about in *Celebrity Spirit Oracle* a few years before. Not long after that, Paul Walker, the actor, came in as well. When we asked why he had brought in Paul's spirit, Johnny simply said that Paul loved fast cars and enjoyed riding with Johnny to our special nights. I had no idea who Paul was until I started to watch his movies that suddenly appeared on TV. I am now a big fan.

Over the years, we had many celebrities come in – well over a hundred in all – and some of them made repeat visits. I can't tell you how excited we were; it was something we had never expected to achieve in the experimental group. When I told my family what was happening, they were also thrilled and wanted all the details about what each celebrity had to say.

Each time a celebrity came to visit, we listened happily as they talked about their lives, gave advice and basically just hung out for a chat. Most were friendly, although a few were not. Some clearly liked to talk and visit often. John Lennon came a few times, swearing a lot. He didn't say much, but he did make us laugh with his direct way of speaking and very funny outlook on things. His Liverpudlian accent was hysterical to listen to.

A few spirits had us in hysterics. We loved listening to the beloved comedian, Joan Rivers. She was so clever, switched-on and witty in spirit, just like she had been in life – a real show-woman and a true entertainer. We all thought Elvis was very sweet.

We were so grateful for the experience; for the chance to meet and talk to all these famous spirits over the years.

Closing the Circle – When Spirit Calls Time

After working for many years in my private séances, I got a message out of the blue from spirit. I heard the voice say: 'Time to close the group down; you have many things to do, and it's time to work in your own space.'

Confused, I opened my eyes from my deep meditation and thought, *okay* ... Trying not to think too much about it, I honoured the suggestion from my spirit guide, White Feather, and rang everyone privately to let them know the sad news.

Once I had informed everyone, I then closed the group over soul and the group energetically. This is something I do when closing all my circles. For example, once a student has moved on, they will no longer be connected to the group, my energy, or my team of spirit guides.

Over the years, I would do this, too, for sitters who never stayed, or were incompatible with the group energy. I must admit this whole process was hard, as the séance group had been a large part of my life for so many years, but I was happy and grateful for the learning I had experienced.

When I left, I took my spiritual tools with me, which were mainly the table and the trumpet I used in all the séances, and placed them in my own healing space and office, at home. The table, which was made for me by one of the kind sitters, is, without a doubt, unique. It is small and round, with two legs. it could spin in both directions – clockwise and anticlockwise – jump in the air, twist and turn, often without anyone touching it, except for the spirit children we worked with.

One day, another physical medium rang me and asked if they could have my spinning spirit table. I told them the group was now closed down, but I was happy to pass the table on to other people, as I felt it would help them. I later discovered that medium had no interest in learning how to use the table, or even following my instructions, which I found disrespectful.

As fate would have it, the energy of the table, and my spirit team for that matter, had other ideas. After a brief disagreement, I realised the error of my ways. My spirit team told me not only was this medium the wrong person, but their disrespect also meant they would never let it happen. One sitter laughed, saying if I had given it to that medium, the table would have exploded, knowing somehow it was going to be used for the wrong intentions.

These days, my beautiful table sits in my office, in memory of those happy times. I have covered it with a children's tablecloth, with love, dedication and blessings, for all the spirit children I feel honoured to have worked with during those wonderful years. The table is a conduit and still holds their loving spirit energy. When I meditate and close my eyes, I can still feel so much loving energy and can imagine their giggles. I understand now I made the right decision out of respect for the dedicated spirits who helped us.

8
UNEXPECTED FAMOUS SPIRIT GUESTS

It takes much dedication and regular sitting to do this work, and the results will not come overnight. It's extremely rewarding, and we've all enjoyed many years of entertainment, and gained insightful information from the spirit world. We also found if the wrong people or energies were sitting in the group, they would soon be moved on, and I believe my spirit team made that happen. It was never personal.

Towards the end of my séances, I decided to keep the group closed and stopped inviting new people. Following this, the energy shifted again and we learnt even more with our group energy, with better rewards.

Through my work in the séance group, I also experienced different types of phenomena which have made their way into my live spirit shows in clubs and other venues. People in the audience will often say they felt someone touch them, or felt a loved one nearby, or saw a chair move by itself. I've also witnessed banging on the walls, lights flickering on and off, and interference with the music or PA system. This type of phenomenon continues to this day.

In the group I ran for years, I brought through the spirits of at least 76 famous icons, without ever knowing who was going to come through on the night. I also sat with a lot of ex-musicians who, like me, loved the music we played, which was mostly rock and music from the 1970s to 1990s.

I have written about some of the spirit guests in this book: Shane Warne, Frank Sinatra, George Harrison, Jimmy Hendrix, Michael Jackson, Janis Joplin, John Belushi. Actors have included Paul Walker, as mentioned earlier; Lucille Ball, who is still very funny over there; and Betty White, who loved animals. After Betty White came in, the spirits of nearly all the sitters' pets came in as well, as if it were a celebration. I had never, in all my years, experienced so many pets from the spirit world.

We've also been visited by Doris Stokes, a British spiritualist, professional medium, and author, on several occasions. When she came through, she always gave instructions through me, the medium, often saying we should pay attention to the cone, which sat on the spinning table, to watch for lights, and to be aware of and feel different types of energy for the spirit phenomena. In one of these sessions, the cone was lifted off the spinning table, and the sitters said they saw a spirit hand very clearly in front of them.

PART TWO

STARS AND CELEBRITIES

P art Two is a compilation of famous icons and celebrities who have appeared in my séances. They are listed alphabetically according to surname, except for Princess Margaret and Queen Elizabeth II.

In addition to each person's astrological sign, I have included their sacred Day number, which provides general insight into their personality, vibration, and energy.

Day numbers are calculated by adding together the digits of the day of birth:

Example: the 14th equals 1 + 4 = 5. *The day number is 5.*

Example: the 29th equals 2 + 9 = 11 = 1 + 1 = 2. *The day number is 2.*

STARS AND CELEBRITIES

Muhammad Ali 74	Val Kilmer. 149
Lauren Bacall. 76	Vivien Leigh. 152
Tammy Faye Baker. 78	John Lennon 154
Lucille Ball 80	Little Richard 157
Jeff Beck 84	Christine McVie 160
John Belushi. 86	Jayne Mansfield 163
Marlon Brando 89	Jim Morrison 166
Karen Carpenter. 92	Bert Newton 169
Sir Sean Connery 95	Dame Olivia Newton-John . 172
Miles Davis 98	Sinead O'Connor 174
Sammy Davis Jr 100	Lisa Marie Presley. 177
John Denver. 103	Princess Margaret 179
Marlene Dietrich. 106	Queen Elizabeth II 181
Harry Edwards 109	Helen Reddy. 183
Farrah Fawcett. 112	Christopher Reeve 185
Roberta Flack 115	Debbie Reynolds 188
Aretha Franklin 118	Alan Rickman. 191
Clark Gable 121	Mickey Rooney. 193
George Harrison 124	Bon Scott 196
Jimi Hendrix 127	Frank Sinatra 198
Katharine Hepburn 129	Anna Nicole Smith. 201
Philip Seymour Hoffman. . 132	Doris Stokes 204
Bob Hope 135	Gloria Swanson 207
Barry Humphries 138	Tina Turner. 210
Marc Hunter 141	Paul Walker. 213
Michael Jackson 143	Shane Warne 215
Janis Joplin 145	Dame Vivienne Westwood . 217
Jack Kerouac. 147	Betty White 220

Muhammad Ali

Born: 17 January 1942, Louisville, Kentucky, United States
Died: 3 June 2016, Scottsdale, Arizona, United States – septic shock due to unspecified natural causes.
Astrological sign: Aquarius
Day number 8: Good businesspeople, know how to make money, self-confident, need to be careful when selecting partners.

Muhammad Ali was an all-American professional boxer, philanthropist and social activist. He was known as the greatest heavyweight boxer of all time. He was a global icon. To many, he was not only the greatest heavyweight boxer, but the greatest sportsman who ever lived. He was a three-time world heavyweight champion.

He refused to serve in the Vietnam War and created a shift in the consciousness of the early 1960s. He campaigned against racism his whole life, criticising Presidential candidate Donald Trump's proposal to ban Muslims from entering the United States. He was famous for saying, 'We as Muslims have to stand up to those who use Islam to advance their own personal agenda.'

For so many people all over the world, Muhammad Ali became an emblem of strength, eloquence, conscience and courage. He was known as a silver-tongued, anti-establishment showman who transcended many barriers.

Before he died, Muhammad Ali developed classic late-stage symptoms of idiopathic Parkinson's. He developed a stooped posture, shuffling steps, postural instability and began falling. He also showed progressive frontal memory impairment consistent with classic Parkinson's.

The séance: When Muhammad Ali came into the séance, the first thing he said after introducing himself was that he was back to himself again and all the illnesses in his body were gone. Then, without wasting any time, he went on to say how much he'd loved his life, and he had lived it to the fullest. He wanted everyone to know how important that belief was to him. He spoke with great pride and passion for what he had achieved, his love for his community and how he never forgot where he came from. He came across as a good person who believed in treating people less fortunate than himself well.

He also said he was lucky to have lived a huge life and lived and breathed when he did. The secret was to believe in yourself, he said, because if you don't, nobody else will. He was proud to help and support people less fortunate than himself. He spoke about his social messages of black pride and black resistance to white domination and acknowledged it was a difficult time in history.

His influence on many of us in the room was very positive. He was a gentle reminder, that everyone should follow their own path and fly.

Words of wisdom

Fight for what you believe in.

I don't count the sit-ups.

Silence is golden when you can't think of a good answer.

It isn't the mountains ahead that wear you down.

I hated every minute of training, but I said, 'Don't quit. Suffer now and live the rest of your life a champion'.

I wish people would love everybody the way they love me.

Float like a butterfly. Sting like a bee. You can't hit what your eyes can't see.

LAUREN BACALL

Born: 16 September 1924, The Bronx, New York, United States
Died: 12 August 2004, New York City, United States – stroke.
Astrological sign: Leo
Day number 7: Spiritual, need to listen to their own intuition, always looking for deeper meanings in life, hang onto things.

Lauren Bacall, the American actress, was named the twentieth greatest female star of classic Hollywood cinema by the American Film Institute. She received an Academy Honorary Award in 2009 in recognition of her contribution to the golden age of motion pictures.

A model before she became a star, she was best known as the provocative glamour queen of cool. She was also well known for her second marriage to a much older man—in fact, twenty-five years her senior—the celebrity, Humphrey Bogart, whom she met through her films. Her films include *To Have and Have Not*, *The Big Sleep* and *Key Largo*, to name a few. She also stared in the comedy *How to Marry a Millionaire* with Marilyn Monroe and Betty Grable. In her later years, Lauren had been a very successful star on Broadway.

Lauren was also known as the 'den mother' of the so-called Hollywood Rat Pack, whose members included Frank Sinatra, Sammy Davis Jr, David Niven, Humphrey Bogart, Judy Garland and others.

The séance: When Lauren came into the séance, she said hello, told the sitters who she was and started talking to them in a matter-of-fact way in her low, husky voice. It was if she was on a stage and entertaining all of us.

She told us her husband, Humphrey Bogart, was her soulmate and he'd taught her a lot about life, love and the ways of the world, which she was eager to learn and very open to. He had taught her so much about her chosen career and was also a good family man when home with the kids. It was obvious she must have adored him. Their romantic and working union—romantic and yet very down to earth—had taught her a lot about herself.

She went on to tell us, in her sassy way, she was always eager to learn from the best of the best and loved to stretch herself in her work, which she loved wholeheartedly. Everything she did had to be real and feel good. Lauren also said she'd smoked a lot and couldn't stop. She would have liked to, but it helped with her nerves, and she continued smoking right up to her passing. She added she'd had little tolerance for idiots or people who wasted her time.

As I channelled her energy, I could feel she sat very tall and straight inside of my energy, and I could feel she had been a very proud and loyal woman, perhaps someone not lost for words. She was a good communicator, but once she'd said what she wanted to say, she was gone.

Words of wisdom

It's perfectly okay to live in a man's world, you know.

I love to love and be loved in return.

Imagination is the highest kite one can fly.

I am not a has-been.

There were times, sure, when I wanted my career to go better.

Legends are all to do with the past and not the present.

You learn to rise above a lot of bad things in your life.

Tammy Faye Baker

Born: 7 March 1942, Minnesota, United States
Died: 20 July 2007, Loch Lloyd, Missouri, United Sates – colon cancer.
Astrological sign: Pisces
Day number 7: Spiritual, need to listen to their own intuition, always looking for deeper meanings in life, hang onto things.

Tammy Faye Baker was an American evangelist, singer, author, talk-show host, recording artist and television personality. She had a love for makeup and played her perky self in TV sitcoms. She also starred in a reality show in which she shared a Hollywood mansion with a former porn star and others. After divorcing her first husband, Jim Baker, while he was behind bars for 'Praise the Lord' Club-related fraud, she married her second husband, Roe Messner. He was later sentenced to jail for three years for bankruptcy fraud.

She was remembered for her glamorous and eccentric personality, as well as her Christian moral views. Many made fun of her and her false eyelashes, but the public loved her in a way they never showed to Jim Baker.

Tammy did great work reaching out to HIV/AIDS patients, especially during the height of the epidemic. She also released three autobiographies during her life. Her motto was, 'You can make it.' She also said, 'You never give up.'

The séance: When Tammy came through, she did so with a big personality and spoke very warmly and sweetly. She said she had been devoted to God her whole life and was a spiritual person. She had truly believed in her faith and her work ever since she was a young girl; it was something very real to her. Her belief in God was everything, she said, and she was elated to preach this to the masses.

She said no matter what had happened, she had always had the strength to lift herself up and keep going. It was her mission to do the work, no matter what. She spoke about how she loved to express herself through singing, and loved entertaining people, which she knew she was good at. She also loved to spread love and faith, as helping people was part of her spiritual contract here on Earth. Her message to all of us was to 'keep the faith always, with everything you do'. She said her faith had helped her with all the incredible highs and lows she consistently experienced throughout her life; it had given her the courage to keep going and not give up.

Words of wisdom

No matter what happens in life, keep the faith, as it keeps you going.

You can educate yourself right out of a relationship with God.

I always say shopping is cheaper than a psychiatrist.

You don't have to be dowdy to be a Christian.

Don't let fear rule your life. Live one day at a time and never be afraid.

Honey, I'm going to my grave with my eyelashes and my makeup on.

Religious people today are courts and juries. When it comes down to it, Jesus died on the cross so we could learn to love others like we love ourselves, not to judge them or persecute them.

LUCILLE BALL

Born: 6 August 1911, Jamestown, New York, United States
Died: 26 April 1989, at Cedars-Sinai Medical Centre, Los Angles, United States – ruptured aortic aneurism.
Astrological sign: Leo
Day number 6: Gentle, caring, home lovers, compassionate, nurturing, family-orientated, magnetic personalities.

Lucille Ball was a very funny American comedian, actress, producer and studio executive. She was a woman before her time, and she will always be remembered as a great pioneer of comedy. Besides being an entertainer, Lucille had many other skills. In her earlier days, she worked as a model, something she said she never enjoyed. She later became the star of her own sitcom TV show, *I Love Lucy*, and starred alongside her husband, Desi Arnaz. The show was very successful, and she was loved by people all over the world.

Not only was she the star of her own show, but she also broke the barrier for women in entertainment. Lucille was the first woman to run a major television studio, Desilu Productions, which produced many TV series, such as *Mission Impossible* and *Star Trek*. She was one of the few people to believe in such projects and willing to give them a go. She had a very good nose for business and was very switched on when it came to artistic ideas.

Besides winning many awards, Lucille has two stars on the Hollywood Walk of Fame. She was recognised by *Time* magazine as being one of the most influential women of the 20th century.

She won five Primetime Emmy Awards and was the recipient of several other accolades, such as the Golden Globe Cecil B. DeMille Award.

The séance: When Lucille first came through in a séance, all the sitters gasped, as she was very well known and loved. Most of us in the group had grown up with her, watching all the old black-and-white TV sitcoms on a regular basis as kids. If anyone could make you laugh, it was Lucille. Everyone loves comedy, as it will always raise the energy and is wonderful for the soul, no matter what we're going through.

It was exciting to have her as our guest. When she started coming through, I could hear the sitters all saying they had loved her as kids, so naturally the room was charged with energy, and everyone was impatient to hear what she had to say. As she was such a popular guest, she ended up visiting us a few times over the years. She said she thought we were progressive and she loved the idea.

Throughout the last session with her, Lucille kept saying how happy she was to be there again. She started talking about how much she had loved her work and pushed herself constantly. Laughing, she said she'd been a workhorse and always had so many ideas. She then said, when we love something very deeply it will always grow. That, she reminded us, is how she accomplished what she wanted; she told us this every time I spoke with her.

Lucille also spoke about having a lot of energy, and how she hated not doing anything. Her mind was always perfecting everything, including her jokes; the one thing she loved was making people laugh. The fact that she could make people laugh really gave her a buzz. Lucille always talked about her achievements, and how she had lived to perform and dance. Throughout the sessions, she said funny things and had the sitters laughing and giggling. It was easy to see she loved an audience. I'm sure she went to a lot of trouble perfecting this, as she was so good at it.

She said she'd been thrilled to do the work she had throughout her life. She'd always made sure she had artistic control, worked with the right people, and kept going, no matter what. Her secrets for success were to never give up, be open to change, try different things and know that nothing in the world is ever too difficult. Also, trust that your co-stars are with you all the way. She said having her own power was something she'd really fought for; it was important for women, especially in her time.

When asked about love, she told us all what a womaniser her husband had been, and the disappointment she'd felt at not being able to control it. It made her very unhappy, and her way of handling this had been to keep working and not stop. Her husband's cheating and dishonest ways with women had affected her deeply, but she'd learned to let it go, forgiving him in the end. She said she loved him, no matter what.

Lucille was full of energy, love and compassion, and spoke very directly. She was happy to be in our energy and was a great communicator, as she had been in life.

Words of wisdom

I'd rather regret the things I've done than things I have not.

Love yourself first and everything else falls into line.

I'm not funny.

Keep the show going, no matter what the odds.

Comedy can be so very healing, and on bad days work is the best medicine.

I think knowing what you cannot do is more important than knowing what you can do.

One of the things I learned the hard way was that it doesn't pay to get discouraged.

I don't know anything about luck.

The secret saying of staying young is to live honestly, eat slowly and lie about your age.

Jeff Beck

Born: 24 June 1944, Wallington, New Jersey, United States
Died: 10 January 2023, in East Sussex, England, United Kingdom – bacterial meningitis.
Astrological sign: Cancer
Day number 6: Gentle, caring, home lovers, compassionate, nurturing, family-orientated, magnetic personalities.

Jeff Beck was an English professional musician and guitarist. He rose to prominence with the band The Yardbirds, after which he formed his own group..He was often called one of the most influential lead guitarists in rock and was one of the top three guitarists in the world, after Jimmy Hendricks and Eric Clapton. He was a master guitarist and had a unique and innovative sound using audio feedback and distortion on his guitar. His releases over the years spanned genres and styles, ranging from blues, rock, hard rock and jazz fusion to a blend of guitar-rock and electronica.

He received the Grammy Award for Best Rock Instrumental Performance six times, and Best Pop Instrumental Performance once. Not surprisingly, he was inducted into the Rock & Roll Hall of Fame—twice.

The séance: When Jeff came into the séance, we were all thrilled as many of the sitters have been musicians at some time in their life and we were all fans. Without a doubt, Jeff was one of the greats. As we heard him speak through me, very softly yet directly, I felt honoured. I felt like I was talking to somebody who had a great gift and was driven by the passion and love to create and work with that gift in every way possible.

He said that when it came to his work, he didn't like to waste time or muck around, and if things weren't right, he would work until things were the way he wanted. He told us there'd been many more projects he'd wanted to explore with other musicians like himself before he died; he said he'd still had so much more to give and learn. He said his guitar had been his passion, and every time he'd played it had been another new experience that had made him feel alive.

Jeff said he'd used his music to explore his feelings and the way he felt about everything going on in the world. It had been the way he expressed himself truly. He said quite often he would go into another space, where he would feel like he was channelling music from other realities and places because his sounds were unique.

Words of Wisdom

I play the way I do because it allows me to come up with the sickest sounds possible. That's the point, isn't it?

If you have a good ear and a bit of talent for music, use it.

I don't care about the rules; I was going to write an autobiography once.

Free yourself from all the negative shackles, which are really not there, and go with the natural flow within.

The world is always waiting for another song. No pressure.

I cherish my privacy and woe betide anyone who tries to interfere with that.

John Belushi

Born: 24 January 1949, Chicago, Illinois, United States
Died: 5 March 1982, Los Angeles, California, United States – drug overdose.
Astrological sign: Aquarius
Day number 6: Gentle, caring, home lovers, compassionate, nurturing, family-orientated, magnetic personalities.

John Belushi was an American comedian, actor, singer and musician. He was best known as one of the seven most popular cast members of *Saturday Night Live* in its first season. He also had a partnership with Dan Aykroyd, whom he met while working in comedy. The two men went on to form the popular Blues Brothers band. John developed a series of characters, imitating Henry Kissinger and Beethoven, and starred in films including *The Blues Brothers* and *National Lampoon's Animal House*.

Throughout his career, John had problems with his health because of his drug use, which got out of control, and he was banned from the *Saturday Night Live* set, only to be rehired again. He was warned by friends and work colleagues of an early death, but he had many addictions including to cocaine and heroin.

He was posthumously honoured with a star on the Hollywood Walk of Fame for his short career, and his family — including his widow and childhood sweetheart, Judith — farewelled him with a traditional Armenian Orthodox Christian funeral.

The séance: When speaking with John, the first thing he said was he could not remember dying. He was sorry and ashamed of his stupidity with drugs and regretted it because he'd still had so much to do. So many people around him had warned him, he said, but it all fallen on deaf ears. After a pause, he said he remembered a woman in the room who had helped him with the hit and that was all. He'd always known he would die young; he had never seen himself as an old man. He had tried many times to have a straight life, and there were periods when he had managed that, only to go back down again; his addiction had been so strong he was simply unable to give up the drugs.

He said performing had been his life and his happy place, especially during the band days. He laughed and said it had been wild at times. He'd loved to dance and go crazy, and he also loved that people thought he was funny. Music was a blast; he'd loved nothing more than to rock and roll.

When he started to become famous and be known as the funny man, it had made him feel proud because he'd worked so hard. A straight job had never been on the agenda, as he'd always felt he was never a traditional man. Even at a young age, he had loved to muck around, make people laugh and have lots of fun. It had made him feel good. He also loved to gather people together and try to help them with their creative projects. He loved the buzz, he said. He always had so many ideas.

Words of Wisdom

Back in Chicago, all we cared about was rock and roll and staying out of the army.

I give so much pleasure to so many people. Why can't I get some pleasure myself?

Nothing is over until we decide it is. Was it over when the Germans bombed Pearl Harbor? Hell, no!

I guess happiness is not a state you want to be in all the time.

I owe it to little chocolate donuts.

It's all false pressure. You put the heat on yourself; you get it from the networks and record companies and movie studios. You put more pressure on yourself to make everything that much harder.

Some comedians love their characters. I don't fall in love with mine. In fact, I get tired of them very fast. You have to be willing to throw them away.

Marlon Brando

Born: 3 April 1924, in Omaha,
Nebraska, United States
Died: 1 July 2004, in Los Angeles, California,
Unite States – respiratory failure.
Astrological sign: Aries
Day number 3: Builders of the world, highly creative,
have an eye for beauty, hard workers.

Marlon Brando was raised by an authoritarian father. As a boy, his emotional needs were dismissed, leaving him in constant search of approval that rarely came, giving him a rebellious streak. He went on to become a well-known film actor – winning an Academy Award twice, as well as a director and an activist. A sex symbol, he married three times and fathered eleven children. He was also open about his bisexuality.

He is regarded as one of the most influential actors of the 20th century, even though it was said he was very difficult to work with. From his acting training with the well-respected Stella Alder Studio of Acting, he was regarded as bringing the 'Stanislavski' system of acting, or method acting, to mainstream audiences. (This is a technique encourages the actor to explore both internal and external aspects, to fully realise the character being portrayed.)

One of Marlon's most famous films was the adaptation of the Tennessee Williams play, *A Streetcar Named Desire*. He's probably best known for his performance in Francis Ford Coppola's *The Godfather* but was also known for his performances in *On the Waterfront* and *The Last Tango in Paris*. He will always be remembered for his incredible performances in everything he did.

When he died, Marlon was known as a rebellious prodigy who had electrified a generation and forever transformed the art of screen acting, but whose obstinacy and eccentricity kept him from fully realising the promise of his early genius.

The séance: When Marlon came through in the group séance, he said he was excited to be in the energy. He told us how he loved his craft as he had always wanted to be an actor, even though there were times when he was too lazy to learn the script. He said he'd worked hard but was his own worst enemy.

As a method actor, he loved being in full character, which he would practise for days as it was essential for him to fully know the character he was playing, inside and out. He said he was a perfectionist and loved to get right into the role; he always became somebody else, never himself, with his own personality and many problems left at the door. He said it was a good way to escape. He wanted to be known for his work.

Each time he was asked a question by the control, and he spoke through me, he would pause, as if finding the right words. He spoke very softly and quietly, sometimes mumbling his words, but making sure he communicated properly.

He told us he went to acting school in The Bronx and about his fond memories of those wonderful days. He spoke fondly about his favourite role being Vito Corleone in *The Godfather* and said he thought Marilyn Monroe was 'a crazy broad'. We all learnt from Marlon how important it is to follow your passion, and with dedication and focus, you can achieve a lot in life.

WORDS OF WISDOM

Nobody tells me what to do. I do things my way.

Never allow yourself to feel anything, because you always feel too much.

Acting is the expression of a neurotic impulse. It's a bum's life. The principal benefit acting has afforded me is the money to pay for my psychoanalysis.

The more sensitive you are, the more certain you are to be brutalised, develop scabs and never evolve.

Privacy is not something that I'm merely entitled to, it's an absolute prerequisite.

The only thing an actor owes his public is not to bore them.

Karen Carpenter

Born: 2 March 1950, New Haven, Connecticut, United States
Died: 4 February 1983, Downey, California, United States – congestive heart failure and complications from anorexia nervosa.
Astrological sign: Aquarius
Day number 2: Peacemakers, intuitive, spiritual, sensitive, may suffer from mood swings.

Karen Carpenter was a well-respected and famous American musician. She was a natural contralto, with an amazing three-octave range, and a drummer with the highly successful band The Carpenters, which she formed with her older brother, Richard. In her younger years, she studied drums in high school and joined the Long Beach State Choir. Her vocal skills were so good that in 2010 *Rolling Stone* magazine listed her as one of the hundred greatest singers of all time. Her genre was pop, easy listening, soft rock and jazz.

Karen worked hard, and after several years of touring, The Carpenters were signed to A&M Records, achieving commercial success throughout the 1970s. As the band progressed, Karen gradually became the front woman and played less drums.

In 1975, Karen became sick from a combination of personal problems and the pressure of work and fame. She developed eating disorders and body dysmorphia –an overwhelming preoccupation with a perceived flaw in one's physical appearance. She was admired by many artists, including Olivia Newton-John, Petula Clark, Dionne Warwick, Dorothy Hamill, as well as John Lennon, who admired her voice.

When she died, she was dressed in a rose-coloured suit in a white, open casket. After Karen's death at such an early age, her brother Richard continued working, releasing several solo albums.

The séance: As I tuned into Karen's spirit energy, I could feel her softness and sensitivity. She spoke very gently and slowly and was happy to talk to me and the sitters. She talked happily about her music, saying how much she loved it and that she had always wanted to be a performer, ever since she was a young girl. The fame that came with it, however, was another story. She said at times she couldn't believe how much their band, The Carpenters, had achieved. She said she was always thrilled to meet other musicians like herself and was overwhelmed at times when they praised her.

We got the impression Karen, although a talented artist, was very humble. When asked about her love life, she spoke about her short-term marriage, something she had not liked to talk about when alive. From the way she spoke so sadly, we all gathered she felt she shouldn't have rushed into the relationship, which hadn't lasted long. She said she had been young and was swept off her feet. He had come across as very charming and it was only later that she found out what he was really like. The marriage had been complicated. Her husband had been very controlling. She hadn't wanted to admit he wasn't nice to her, which hadn't helped her mental health and wellbeing. She also said nobody – friends or family – liked him, saying he wasn't the man for her. All she'd ever wanted was to have love in her life, a good career and a happy family.

She was grateful for her success as a musician but was sad over her failure in the romance department. The last part of her life had been sad. She felt as though a dark cloud hung over her, her illness was a constant battle, and the demons in her head were never far away. Still, she carried on, wanting to work and live her best life.

Before she went, she said that in spirit she was with her dog, who was like her child, and had found peace and was happy.

Words of Wisdom

Not enough people in the world are happy.

I'm determined to be contented, and having plenty of money from working makes it easier for me.

The image we have would be impossible for Mickey Mouse to maintain. We're just normal people.

I may not be in control of anything else, but I am in control of my body.

It's kind of nice to be remembered by your peers and your fans, because you can achieve a lot of success and be a creep, too. But we try to be nice, just normal people.

I have a harder time finding somebody.

People never think of entertainers as being human.

Sir Sean Connery

Born: 25 August 1930, Edinburgh, Scotland, United Kingdom
Died: 31 October 2020, The Bahamas – with dementia, in his sleep.
Astrological sign: Virgo
Day number 7: Spiritual, need to listen to their own intuition, always looking for deeper meanings in life, hang onto things.

Sean Connery was a celebrated and renowned Scottish actor whose career spanned many years. He was probably best remembered as being the first Scottish actor to portray the fictional, formidable British agent James Bond. He starred in seven Bond films between 1962 and 1983: *Dr. No, From Russia with Love, Goldfinger, Thunderball, You Only Live Twice, Diamonds Are Forever* and *Never Say Never Again.* He also worked with Alfred Hitchcock, director of the film *Marnie.* Other directors he worked with were Sidney Lumet and John Hudson. His last film role was in *The League of Extraordinary Gentlemen.*

He received many awards for his acting skills, including the Academy Award for Best Supporting Actor for his role in *The Untouchables.*

His first marriage was to the Australian film star and actress, Diane Cilento. He was married to his second wife, Micheline Roquebrune, for over forty years.

He has a plaque near the site of his birth in Fountainbridge, Edinburgh.

The séance: It was thrilling to talk to Sean, who was by far my favourite James Bond. It was amazing when he came through in a meditation and I channelled him, listening very carefully to what he had to say. The news I was writing a new book must have been out there in the spirit world, but this is an example of what happens in my world and it's always exciting.

The first thing I heard when I closed my eyes was his Scottish voice. He said his name and started talking straightaway about how serious he'd been about his work. My impression was he was a perfectionist and took his work very seriously. He said he had worked hard on his career his whole life. He hadn't wanted to be stereotyped into one character—particularly the character of 007—as he was afraid people wouldn't take him seriously. He said looking back, he'd enjoyed the role, and he laughed at how people saw him as a sex symbol back in the day, when his intention had just been to make the character believable.

He also said he was a 'man's man', liked fast cars, excitement, good food and a drink or two. He'd always loved the energy and nature of Scotland. It was too cold to live there, he said, laughing, and then he proudly showed me the Highlands; pictures of mountains and peaks appeared in my mind.

Sean also said he saw himself as a simple person, with good taste in the best of things, and was chuffed with his own success. He appreciated the experience he'd had, with the travelling and the people he'd worked with along the way, as there was always a story.

When I asked him about his love life, he didn't say much, except to say his second wife, Micheline, had given him a lot of comfort, and there had been no drama, which he hadn't tolerated from people. He said she was a strong woman who had a very soothing effect on him and loved him deeply.

WORDS OF WISDOM

I like women. I don't understand them, but I like them.

Laughter kills fear, and without fear there can be no faith. For without fear of the devil there is no need for God.

There is nothing like a challenge to bring out the best in a man.

Don't let someone else's opinion of you become your reality.

If you're not a positive energy, you're a negative energy.

Do the best you can.

If you can dream it, you can do it.

MILES DAVIS

Born: 26 May 1926, in Alton, Illinois, United States
Died: 28 September 1991, Santa Monica, California, United States – stroke and respiratory problems.
Astrological sign: Gemini
Day number 8: Good businesspeople, know how to make money, self-confident, need to be careful when selecting partners.

Miles Davis was an African American trumpeter, bandleader and composer, one of the most influential and acclaimed figures in the history of jazz. In his five-decade career, he managed and adopted a variety of musical directions, which kept him at the forefront of many major stylistic developments in the world of jazz. In the 1950s, he became addicted to heroin, which greatly affected his ability to perform. In 1954, he overcame his drug addictions. That year, his performance of the song 'Round Midnight' at the Newport Jazz Festival in Rhode Island, earned him a recording contract with Columbia Records.

After a period of ill health and a five-year retirement, he returned to music in the 1980s, working with young musicians and incorporating pop influences. During this time, he became very commercial and was recognised for his years of work. He went on to perform sold-out concerts all over the world, while branching out into visual arts, film and television work. His work was his art and his life, the way he saw it. He was one of the most influential, brilliant and acclaimed musicians of his time, which kept him in the public eye in the music and jazz world.

The séance: When Miles came into the séance to visit us, we were all excited as many of the sitters, plus myself, were musicians. I couldn't get over how his energy was very similar to what I'd witnessed when I actually saw him perform before his death. I knew without a doubt that it was definitely him. When he spoke through the medium, his words were very clear and precise. He came across as very humble and gentle, and mostly spoke about his music and how it was his art. He lived and breathed his work, he said, and it helped him through difficult times in his life, which he said were quite a few.

The whole experience was amazing. When he was alive, Miles's music had been powerful and uplifting. It was no wonder we were all giggles and starstruck, including myself; he had indeed been a grand master in his day. He didn't say much but instead seemed to watch us and what we were doing. When asked, he said we were all unusual. Towards the end, he laughed and said he was enjoying his time with us. Then suddenly he was gone.

I later wondered if Miles had had an interest in the supernatural. If he had, I wouldn't be surprised. Perhaps the next time he comes through he'll have more to say.

Words of Wisdom

Live to create, create to live. When you wake up each day, this is your purpose.

The thing to judge in any jazz artist is, does the man project, and does he have ideas?

A legend is an old man with a cane known for what he used to do.

I'll play it first then tell you what it is later.

Do not fear mistakes.

Don't play what's there, play what's not there.

If you sacrifice your art because of some woman, or some man, or for some colour, or for some wealth, you can't be trusted.

Sammy Davis Jr

Born: 8 December 1925, Harlem,
New York, United States
Died: 16 May 1990, Beverly Hills, California,
United States – laryngeal cancer.
Astrological sign: Sagittarius
Day number 8: Good businesspeople, know how to
make money, self-confident, need to
be careful selecting partners.

S ammy Davis Jr was an American singer, dancer, actor, comedian, recording artist, photographer and activist. He was called the greatest entertainer ever to grace a stage in the United States. At age two, Sammy began his career in vaudeville with his father, Sammy Davis Sr, and the Will Mastin Trio, which toured nationally. His film career began in 1933.

His nickname was Mr Show Business, and he called himself the only black, Puerto Rican, one-eyed Jewish entertainer in the world. Following a near-fatal car crash, he reflected deeply on his existence and, after meeting a Jewish chaplain who called his survival a miracle, converted to Judaism. And after learning more about Judaism, he felt Jews and black people shared a similar history of oppression.

He recorded dozens of albums, appeared on TV, in Broadway shows and films. He was known as one of the greatest pop-culture icons in the world. He was also a key member of the famous Rat Pack and a good friend of Frank Sinatra, who was like a big brother. During his career he toured internationally with Dean Martin, Frank Sinatra and Liza Minnelli.

The séance: When Sammy came into the séance, he seemed to have a very big personality for someone who, while in the living, had been quite small in stature. He sounded excited to visit us and kept saying so. He spoke about the trouble being a man of colour, his difficult relationships with the mob and how other people would make it their business to interfere with his private affairs, including his love life. His relationships with white women had always caused him terrible problems.

He was also a member of the famous Rat Pack. The early 1960s version of the group included Frank Sinatra, Dean Martin, Joey Bishop, Peter Lawford, and Shirley Maclaine – its only female member.

He was full of energy and came across as very friendly, spoke very openly and was receptive to much of the questioning. In fact, he seemed to be enjoying talking about himself. He tried to joke with the sitters as he literally bounced around them energetically. Overall, he was a wonderful spirit communicator.

Towards the end of the session, Sammy told us he had been a hard worker in his life, and had always known how important family was, even though he wasn't often around. He also said he was proud of being a black person and his roots. He said he was driven throughout his life to be successful and had made the most out of every opportunity that came his way, telling us to give everything a go and to not let anything, how impossible it seemed, to ever hold you back. This was a great message of inspiration for all of us, with all the trials and tribulations of life.

Words of wisdom

You always have two choices: your commitment versus your fear.

Real success is not on the stage, but off the stage as a human being, and how you get along with your fellow man.

All I really had was my talent.

Reality is never as bad as a nightmare, as the mental tortures we inflict on ourselves.

Talk about handicap. I'm a one-eyed Negro who's Jewish.

The ultimate mystery is oneself.

There are certain romances that belong in certain cities, in a certain atmosphere, in a certain time.

John Denver

Birthname: John Deutchendorf Jr
Born: 31 December 1943, Roswell, New Mexico, United States
Died: 12 October 1997, California, United States – in a plane crash.
Astrological sign: Capricorn
Day number 4: Down to earth, have difficulty making decisions, honest and trustworthy.

John Denver was an American country and folk singer and songwriter, who started playing his grandmother's guitar at eleven. He was one of the most popular, pure acoustic artists of the 1970s. He is remembered by many as one of the most beloved entertainers of his era. His genres were folk, folk rock, pop, country and soft rock.

In his career, he released three hundred songs, writing two hundred of them himself. Most of his music was certified gold, and his heartfelt songs were mostly about nature, real-life experiences and relationships. He also appeared in several films in his life, but singing and performing were his main interests. Three of his most famous songs were 'Rocky Mountain High', 'Take Me Home Country Roads' and 'West Virginia'.

In the 1970s, he also became a passionate and hardworking activist, outspoken on issues such as the environment, poverty, homelessness, hunger, and the African aid crisis. In 1976, he founded the Windstar Foundation, a non-profit organisation supporting sustainable living. With his passionate views, he spoke out against the Ronald Reagan administration and wrote a book about his life and beliefs. In 2024, he was posthumously awarded a star on the Hollywood Walk of Fame.

The séance: When John entered, I was pleasantly surprised. I could feel his gentle nature, strong spiritual and light energy when he came into my body. I sensed he was a cigarette smoker when alive, as I could smell cigarettes all around him. I kept wondering if it helped relax him in some way. The other strange thing was, I could hear the words to his song 'Leaving on a Jet Plane' playing over and over in my head.

I would describe him as a gentle soul, very deep and articulate, but also funny at times. When he started talking about himself, he said he loved to take off in his plane, or 'go off the grid', as he called it, but was disappointed when he crashed. He said the crash came out of the blue and was a big surprise. Everything had happened really fast. He never felt the impact of the crash as he felt his spirit leave his body, then it went black for a while. 'Everything happened so fast,' he kept saying.

Then we asked him about his music. He said he loved what he did with a passion and took his craft very seriously, but he was always aware of the world of politics and what was going on. He wanted to make a difference and help people as much as he could, in his own way.

He said he would think too much about things, which made him want to withdraw from life. I understood this and it made me realise what a complex person he must have been. John said his music had kept his soul happy and was pleased that the songs he sang had healed so many.

When we asked about how he saw the world, he said there was a lot of injustice, and we should fight for what we believed in. The group agreed with this. At the end—he left quite suddenly—we asked if he would visit again. He said yes.

Words of wisdom

I've always liked to think that we put ourselves in the circumstances in life that will support us moving to wherever it is our spirit is going.

Relax, ease back in your seats and let the music take you to wherever it does.

Peace is a conscious choice.

Commit yourself to whatever it is you can contribute in order to create a healthy and sustainable future; the world needs you desperately. Find that in yourself and make a commitment; that is what will change the world.

The future of life on Earth depends on our ability to see the sacred where others see only the common.

Music does bring people together. It allows us to experience the same emotions. People everywhere are the same in heart and spirit. No matter what language we speak, what colour we are, the form of our politics, or the expression of our love and faith, music proves we are the same.

Things go up and down. If you can survive the down, it will come back.

MARLENE DIETRICH

Born: 27 December 1901, Berlin, Germany
Died: 6 May 1922, Paris, France – kidney failure.
Astrological sign: Sagittarius
Day number 9: Imaginative, passionate, creative, have strong spiritual beliefs, like to run their own show, have trouble trusting, need to let go of the things that no longer serve them.

Marlene Dietrich was a charismatic German-American actress and singer, performing both on the stage and in silent films. She was also a prolific smoker. Her career spanned nearly seven decades, and she was well known for her elegance, smouldering sex appeal, distinctive voice and unusual personal style. Her famous performance as Lola in *The Blue Angel* brought her international acclaim and a contract with Paramount Pictures.

A popular star of the 1930s and 1940s, she was also known for her fashionable style and diverse portrayals of women. She was a firm advocate for the American war effort during the Second World War, contributing much of her time, energy and musical talents to aid the American troops. She was a member of what was called 'The sewing circle', a phrase used to describe a collection of quietly lesbian and bisexual actresses in Hollywood.

Some of her films to be remembered are *The Scarlett Empress, Blond Venus, The Blue Angel, Witness for the Prosecution, Shanghai Express* and *The Devil is a Woman*. She was known to be very modern, independent and outspoken for the era. She was famous for her style and penchant for glamorous and androgynous outfits, which made her very different from the rest of the leading ladies at the time. It was widely speculated that her appearance was a political stance as well as a fashion statement, and she was known to wear men's clothes to make the statement she was of no gender.

The séance: When Marlene came into the sitting, some of the sitters had not heard of her because she was a star and siren of yesteryear, but I remembered her from when I was a child. I had always loved the way she came across as a woman of substance – very powerful in her ideologies and beliefs – and who probably would have been an extremely liberated woman based on some of her films. I also remember the turbans she used to wear.

She was a strong spirit with a lot to say. She told us she'd had to fight for what she wanted, and once she'd made up her mind she would never give up. She also said if anybody crossed her, they were finished, as she had no time for other people's stupidity. It was no wonder that when came through, she seemed like a mighty force; she was a strong, independent and beautiful soul who had little patience for stupid people and was born to be an entertainer.

When asked about love, she said she was a strong believer in freedom and loved both men and women. She also spoke about how important it is for women to stand in their power and be accountable; women's intelligence and opinions matter, and they should not have their ideas swept under the carpet in a man's world. This belief resonated with me and is very evident today with the powerful MeToo movement in 2019–2020 about women speaking up about abuse and their rights. She was a strong believer in freedom of speech.

Words of Wisdom

Never admit you're wrong when of course you're right.

Most women set out to try to change a man, and when they have changed him, they don't like him.

I am at heart, a gentleman.

Courage and grace are a formidable mixture.

A king, realising his incompetence, can either delegate or abdicate his duties.

The diaphragm is the greatest invention since pancake makeup.

In America, sex is an obsession; in other parts of the world, it's a fact.

Harry Edwards

Born: 29 May 1893, London, England, United Kingdom
Died: 7 December 1976, London, England, United Kingdom – pneumonia.
Astrological sign: Gemini
Day number 2: Peacemakers, intuitive, spiritual, sensitive, may suffer from mood swings.

In his early career, Harry Edwards worked as a printer and a politician. When attending a meeting at a spiritual church in 1935, he was told by the medium present he had healing powers. After attending the church, he became a well-known spiritual healer worldwide, and people from all walks of life experienced his special powers firsthand. He later became an author.

Many people who are open to the spiritual world and everything it offers, like healing, believed in Harry Edwards and what he has contributed to the world. It is believed by many he was one of the greatest spiritual healers of our time. He was an incredible influence and gave healing and hope to so many. The centre he founded, the Harry Edwards Healing Sanctuary, is still visited by people from all over the world.

Harry's success and fame opened the way for the distance healing practised by healers today. I had read articles about a type of pneumonia being healed, where a bright blue light appeared in people's homes — sometimes filling a room, sometimes glowing on the body — when Harry was asked to send distant or remote healing. I would have loved to witness that myself, which I understand to be simply healing energy travelling across a great distance.

Harry also helped to set up the National Federation of Spiritual Healers, a formal organisation.

The séance: When Harry came into the séance, he spoke in a clear voice and described how his work while on Earth had been simple, safe and supportive—energy therapy aimed to bring balance to mind, body, spirit and soul, as well as to stimulate the body's own natural healing abilities. Harry was passionate about his work and was a big believer in the power and gifts of spirit. He told us that all positive energy, which is love, is good for everyone, no matter what their beliefs are. He added spirit energy never causes any harm, as it is pure unconditional love in its truest form that comes from the higher powers in the universe.

As I practised spiritual healing myself for many years, I also understand its benefits. I also believe any type of alternative and spiritual healing is best used in conjunction with conventional therapies. You don't have to be ill to benefit from spiritual healing, as it also supports good health and spiritual, emotional and physical wellbeing. Harry himself claimed that among his healing team were several deceased scientists working through him and they were complimentary about his healing powers.

Words of Wisdom

The divine power of spirit will always do the work, just remember to get out of the way.

We are all natural conduits of energy, and here to channel universal loving energy to help others who are less fortunate than ourselves.

Don't be afraid to take a leap of faith and surrender to this spiritual calling.

Developing your gifts with the help of a teacher can be a good way to start, as can joining a group of like-minded people.

We often work with spirits from the spirit world who once walked the earth as healers and doctors.

Did you know that friends, animals and birds are attracted to your wonderful loving aura when you encounter them?

It's time to help humanity if you have a healing gift; it's a wonderful gift.

Spiritual healing is a holistic approach to wellbeing that works with the body's energy systems, in conjunction with conventional medicine, to promote physical, emotional and mental balance.

Farrah Fawcett

Born: 2 February 1947, Corpus Christi,
Texas, United States
Died: 25 June 2009, Santa Monica, California,
United States – anal cancer.
Astrological sign: Aquarius
Day number 2: Peacemakers, intuitive, spiritual, sensitive,
may suffer from mood swings.

Farrah Fawcett was an American actress who was known as 'The golden girl'. She was loved unconditionally by her friends and family for her strength, honesty and perseverance. She received a diagnosis of cancer in 2006 and died three years later. Before she died, she created the Farrah Fawcett Foundation with the aim of helping other people with cancer. At the time of her illness, no one talked about cancer, but she made it her mission to break the silence. If nothing else, she wanted to use her fame to help others who were also fighting the disease.

She was also famous for her hairstyle; everyone loved her layered style and every hairdresser in the world tried to copy it.

She was a four-time Primetime Emmy Award nominee and six-time Golden Globe Award nominee, rising to fame in the television series *Charlie's Angels*. Besides appearing in commercials and guest roles in television, she was also remembered for her role in *The Six Million Dollar Man*, in which she appeared with her then-husband, Lee Majors. She also worked off-Broadway. She earned her fourth Emmy nomination for her work as a producer on *Farrah's Story*, a documentary about her battle with cancer.

Her last words were about her son, her greatest love, and she kept repeating his name. After her death, Lee Majors said that Farrah had been 'an angel on Earth and is now an angel in heaven forever'. Ryan O'Neal, Farrah's late husband, is buried next to her.

The séance: When Farrah came through the séance, her energy was enormous, yet so light. She was a strong spirit with a loud voice, and her energy was sweet, gentle and kind, like a beautiful angel. She came across as a compassionate soul who really cared about others and knew what she wanted. She felt very loving. My body tingled, and I knew without a doubt she had a big heart, with loads of, what I felt was, compassion.

When asked by the control if she had anything to share, she said, in a determined voice that she didn't care what people had thought of her in the often-troubled periods, in her later years.

She had a strong, warrior-woman energy that whirled rapidly around the room. She was articulate when she spoke and said she was aware she'd been known as 'The golden girl' for most of her career. She said she'd felt this was a huge responsibility and had been determined to help people in any way she could. She said she was grateful for the amazing experiences she'd had when her star was shining. Nothing had ever stopped her doing what she wanted to do, even when she was sick and in pain; she was always up for the challenge, she said.

The sitters in the room were very taken aback by her visit. As she spoke through the medium, it was obvious to everyone she had wanted to do a lot when she was on Earth, with her passionate energy and determination. We all felt she was a beautiful, courageous soul who loved to help people, no matter what the consequences.

She kept repeating that once she made up her mind about things, she followed through and didn't worry about anything, no matter how big or trivial it was. She said if she was worried, she would keep going and fight for her cause to the end. She said her inner courage had kept her going with everything in her life. Everyone in the group was touched by her kindness, humanity and courage.

Words of Wisdom

No matter what you're going through, never give up or lose hope. Keep going. That way you can help others.

If it feels right, keep going forward with all your projects with a passion.

You have to eventually grow up and take control of your life, which is very hard to do.

You have an inner knowing, so trust your innate superpowers and be courageous in all your undertakings, even though you may feel, sense and taste the fear in your mouth if it rises at certain confusing times.

If you're a spiritual person, just remember the gift of prayer is amazing. It's a direct line to the spirit world and the angelic kingdom, where the spirits are only too happy to assist you when you ask them. Just thank them afterwards with great gratitude.

Ask yourself what this experience is teaching you.

Honour and love your spirit and truth always, and you will always be looked after.

God gave women intuition and femininity. Used properly, the combination easily jumbles the brain of any man I've ever met.

Everything has positive and negative consequences.

ROBERTA FLACK

Born: 10 February 1937, Black Mountain, North Carolina, United States
Died: 24 February 2025, New York City, United States – cardiac arrest, a complication of ALS (Lou Gehrig's disease).
Astrological sign: Pisces
Day number 1: Born leaders, independent, ambitious, hardworking, prefer to work on their own rather than with others, can be stubborn.

Roberta Flack was an African-American rhythm and blues singer known for her great hits, 'The First Time Ever I Saw Your Face' and 'Killing Me Softly with His Song'. She was also known for her duets with soul singer Donny Hathaway.

As a child prodigy, she played piano in the church from an early age. During her teenage years, she trained as a concert pianist, harbouring a special affection for composers such as Bach, Schumann and Chopin. At the age of fifteen, she obtained a full scholarship to study music at Howard University, where she met her friend and future duet partner, Donny Hathaway. Finally coming into her power, she also began to sing and did so well that she was able to give up teaching.

Roberta's first album, *First Take*, was a major breakthrough for her, and led quickly to stardom. Her breakthrough came when jazz pianist Les McCann heard her perform and sent a tape of her music to Atlantic Records. She wrote and produced her albums, won a Grammy Award and was honoured with a star on the Hollywood Walk of Fame. Before she died, she performed in a wheelchair.

The séance: Tuning into Roberta was a beautiful experience. I had watched a documentary on her life years ago and loved her music. I could feel her strong mind and body in spirit when she came close to me. When asked about her life, she said she was a private person, and music had taken her to another world. Her work was how she had expressed herself. She said whatever she played, no matter what it was, she would always make it her own.

Roberta said her musical talent was something she was born with; it was her main driver, and she'd wanted to explore it, no matter what. She never saw herself as a housewife, but an independent spirit with a lot to do. Driven by her music, she said she was happy to travel anywhere in her tireless pursuit of discovery.

When I asked her about her duets with Donny Hathaway, she said he was on her level in so many ways, and they'd also had a strong connection on a soul level. She'd known he was unwell, but they managed to keep it together and create incredible music. She said he was wonderful to work with.

She said later in her life she'd been friends with her neighbours, John Lennon and Yoko Lennon. They were all very good friends and spent time together. John Lennon's sudden death was something like Donny's death; it took her a while to get over.

Words of wisdom

Remember, always walk in the light. And if you feel like you're not walking in it, go find the light. Love the light.

There is a river somewhere that flows through the lives of everyone.

So, see every opportunity as golden, and keep your eyes on the prize—yours, not anybody else's.

Getting married is easy. Staying married is more difficult. Staying happily married for a lifetime is among the fine arts.

Music comes from my heart and then goes upstairs to my head where I check it out.

The first time I saw your face, I thought the sun rose in your eyes.

Strumming my pain with his fingers, singing my life with his words, killing me softly with his song.

Aretha Franklin

Born: 25 March 1942, Memphis, Tennessee, United States
Died: 16 August 2018, Detroit, Michigan, United States – pancreatic cancer.
Astrological sign: Aries
Day number 7: Spiritual, need to listen to their own intuition, always looking for deeper meanings in life, hang onto things.

Aretha Franklin was an American soul singer, songwriter and activist. She was the iconic musical feminist who ordered her man to show her some respect way back in the 1960s. After that, no one messed with her, and she was ordained 'The Queen of Soul'. *Rolling Stone* magazine crowned her the Greatest Singer of All Time. Some of her greatest hits include 'Respect', 'I Say a Little Prayer' and 'A Natural Woman'.

From an early age, Aretha learnt some hard lessons. Her mother died of a heart attack when she was nine, and it was said that her father, a renowned preacher with a gospel caravan, had wandered through his marriage with many infidelities.

Aretha found herself pregnant at the age of twelve to a local boy she met through her father's church, where she sang in the choir. Her first child was a child with special needs, and she was known to be a devoted mother, even though she struggled as a working professional singer.

One of her proudest moments was receiving the Presidential Medal of Freedom at the White House. She also received a Pulitzer Prize citation for her 'indelible contribution to American Music and culture for over five decades'. The memory of her greatness in the world will always be remembered.

The séance: When she came into the séance, Aretha's strong spirit could be felt by all the sitters. She had a huge energy, which everyone in the room felt. It was no wonder she was an enigma when she died. When she spoke through the medium, her words were strong and breathtakingly powerful, which gave us all so much inspiration.

Aretha told us that while on Earth, she had continued, no matter what the consequences, to keep marching forward with what she believed was important in her life, for herself and others. She then said it was her faith that got her through things. It had not been easy, with all the many tests, trials and tribulations she had endured, and her journey was often painful. She admitted at times it had been a real struggle, but her faith in God was her superpower. She went on to say she'd had a great belief in her talent, as if God had placed her on Earth for a mission.

The whole room was in a state of calmness, and every single person present at the séance sat spellbound as her incredible, powerful love for everyone in the room went continually around in circles. Finally, the medium was asked to come back into her body, and the energy was closed down.

Aretha's messages about her life were simple, yet regal, full of love and spoken with few words. Everyone in the room was affected by her very humble messages, and in total awe, feeling that they were in the electric energy of a great presence. She told us she always felt she was born to open people's hearts and souls with her incredible healing voice, and messages of inspiration and love.

Words of wisdom

Believe in yourself, girl, even if nobody else does. You got God on your side, so you have this.

You have the power.

Find your life's spiritual purpose as soon as you can, and over time everything will open up the way it's meant to.

Know who you are, so believe and receive.

We all have lessons we can learn from, so don't get stuck on the road, move on.

Stick to the plan and your life will open up.

Believe, and ask spirit for what you need.

Embrace change always; never be afraid, as change is a good thing.

God has a mission for all of us, in every aspect of our lives.

Enjoy love while it's in your life. It's a gift and don't forget to smother it with a whole lot of gratitude.

Clark Gable

Born: 1 February 1901, Ohio, United States
Died: 16 November 1960, Hollywood, California, United States – heart attack.
Astrological sign: Capricorn
Day number 1: Born leaders, independent, ambitious, hardworking, prefer to work on their own than with others, can be stubborn.

Oscar winner, Clark Gable, a Hollywood legend from the golden age of Hollywood, starred in over sixty films. His father always opposed his son's decision to become an actor, and even after Clark became a major star his father still denounced acting as a 'sissy' occupation. Clark went on to become one of the most consistent box-office performers in the history of Hollywood. He was a big star and was referred to by many as the 'King of Hollywood' for his thirty-seven-year career and his leading roles.

Starting out as an extra in films, he progressed in his career and eventually moved to Metro-Goldwyn-Mayer. He won an Academy Award in 1934. He is best known for his Oscar-winning performance in the epic movie *Gone with the Wind*, in which he starred with Vivien Leigh. In the movie he played the character of Rhett Butler, an unforgettable tough guy and all-time charmer of ladies.

His biggest fear was of flying, which probably came from his involvement in the Second World War, and he made the long journeys across the United States by train. He was fond of Marilyn Monroe, who had a childhood crush on him and held a suspicion he might be her father – a claim Clark said was nonsense.

The séance: When Clark came through into the séance through the medium with his soft American drawl, everyone clapped in appreciation; it was exciting for him to visit us from the golden age of Hollywood. It was so strange, though, because when he spoke through me, the medium, he sounded very down to earth. His language was very simple, ordinary and polite, and he sounded nothing like the tough, manly characters he played in his films, who were mostly swashbuckling heroes.

As the séance went on, it gradually felt like we were talking to a kind, ordinary gentleman, but from an older era, as he was so polite and considerate when asked questions by the control. We were all taken aback by this, but he was understandably humble, because he had had a big life, with many incredible highs and lows – something many people don't experience in a lifetime. Clark lived his life well, was aware of the trappings of Hollywood, and spoke about his great love for Carol Lombard, his soulmate, who he was overjoyed to have met.

Clark told us the story of how, when working on a film, he almost walked off the set when he discovered the studio facilities were segregated and signposted for whites and coloureds. Segregation was something he did not believe in.

He said several times he was grateful for everything he had experienced in life, and didn't mind being described as a strong, outspoken masculine man, well respected in his field, and always the gentleman, no matter the odds.

Words of wisdom

Whatever you do, learn to swim in your own lane.

Stay true to your beliefs and don't be afraid to stand up and say them.

Nobody likes a coward. Take responsibility for your actions; they speak louder than words.

I'm a team player, for sure, but I like to run my own show. I don't like to be controlled, as it never works.

You have to try love at least once in your life. If you don't, you've never lived.

Don't hang on to resentment. It never gets you anywhere; it just eats you up from the inside.

Don't ever discuss women with anyone at all. What happens in the bedroom stays there.

George Harrison

Born: 25 February 1943, Liverpool,
England, United Kingdom
Died: 29 November 2001, Los Angeles,
California, United States – lung cancer.
Astrological sign: Pisces
Day number 7: Spiritual, need to listen to their own intuition, always looking for deeper meanings in life, hang onto things.

When George Harrison was thirteen, he bought his first guitar and befriended Paul McCartney at their school. He was an English musician, singer and music and film producer who achieved international fame as the lead guitarist of one of the most famous bands in the world, The Beatles. A very spiritual Pisces, he was known as the quiet Beatle.

George's strongest relationship in the band was with John Lennon, who he respected and idolised for his talent. George spent as much time as possible with John. Later on, a factor in the split of The Beatles was Harrison's growth as a composer in the second half of the Beatles' career. Many of his song ideas were rejected by Lennon and McCartney, especially from 1968.

He also introduced Indian musical influences, most notably through his use of Indian instruments and his interest in Hindu-aligned spirituality on The Beatles' albums. He became a great devotee of Eastern spirituality almost overnight and spoke about his passion for it. It continued to influence his music and his views on life when he went out on his own.

Two years before he died, George survived a knife attack by an intruder at his home.

The séance: George came through early one morning in my office, out of the blue. I was in a deep meditation and then a trance state when it happened. All I can say is, it was as if time stood still as a very calm and big, big energy entered the room and sat in my energy. As I closed my eyes and tuned into him, I heard his music running softly through my mind; the song 'My Sweet Lord' kept playing over and over in my head. It was totally strange, but beautiful, as I hadn't heard that song in a very long time. As his music played, I could feel my heart flutter a couple of times as I thought about my old memories of his music and words. I was big fan of his music in my early years, so it was an amazing experience.

I couldn't help thinking George must have been a very private person in the living, as he came to talk to me alone and not in the séance with my sitters or the control.

With my eyes closed, I then began to see an image of his face from his younger years, with a big smile on it. This made me think how enlightened he must have been at the time in his life when he discovered spirituality. I also smelled sweetly perfumed flowers in the room, which reminded me of angels.

When I asked George if he had some messages, he said in a gentle voice, he had lived the best life and was amazed and perplexed at how he had experienced such golden and incredible opportunities, for which he would always be grateful. He then went on to say that his belief in spiritual matters had been a turning point in his life and had changed him greatly. His favourite mantra that had helped him was chanting, 'Hari Krishna, Hari Krishna, Hari Krishna'; he said it had helped clear and expand his energy and heart.

Whatever George is doing in the spirit world now, I'm sure it includes helping humanity. It was a truly beautiful experience. George teaches us to go within and meditate to find the outcomes for our journey.

Words of Wisdom

There is always a deeper spiritual purpose; it's the way to your soul's salvation.

Quite often in life we will come to a crossroads where we look for a new meaning or purpose to what life presents us, which is much more than the boring day to day.

When you work with the spiritual path you understand there is a deeper meaning to life.

Like a butterfly emerging from a cocoon, meditation will take you to a higher level of consciousness, true happiness, peace and an incredible feeling of being with one with everyone and everything around you.

Everything else can wait, but the search for God cannot wait, and love one another.

We are not these bodies, but souls having a bodily experience.

True love is something I did have the fortune to discover.

Jimi Hendrix

Born: 27 December 1942, Seattle,
Washington, United States
Died: 18 September 1970, London, England,
United Kingdom – from complications
related to a barbiturate overdose.
Astrological sign: Capricorn
Day number 9: Imaginative, passionate, creative, have
strong spiritual beliefs, like to run their own
show, have trouble trusting, need to let go
of the things that no longer serve them.

Jimi Hendrix was an iconic American: he was a blues guitarist, songwriter and singer, and was admired by the masses. In elementary school, he discovered he had perfect pitch, the ability to identify notes by name, and to photographically remember songs in key. In 1967, he made his first appearance at the Monterey Pop Festival with his band, the Jimi Hendrix Experience, and quickly became established as a rock superstar in front of massive crowds.

He often did the same gigs as his friend, Janis Joplin, and they would sometimes meet backstage. He also met up with Mick Jagger of the Rolling Stones at the *Top of the Pops* studio in 1967.

His bandmates nicknamed him The Bat because of his nocturnal lifestyle; he often stayed up late partying, then hibernated inside all the next day, like a bat, with the curtains closed.

In 1969, he was the highest-paid rock star musician and headlined the Isle of Wight Festival in 1970. Even though he was part of the music world for such a short time, Jimi is still widely regarded, including by fellow musicians, as one of the greatest and most popular guitarists in history.

The séance: When Jimi came through, he spoke through the medium in a very quiet, humble voice. We all had the sense of how fragile he was; he seemed to be a free soul, yet his energy felt almost frail. He said he was a creative mind, and he spoke very carefully when he described his life. I also felt him to be quite intuitive and a deep thinker. He said he may have been naïve at certain times, especially when it came to trusting the wrong people, like some of the groupies and fake people, and about his manager in particular, who had never really looked after him and had taken advantage of him for financial gain.

When the control asked him about the murder allegations, he said he'd had some bad people after him at the time, but it was his own carelessness, tiredness, lack of boundaries and ill health that had let him down in the end; all the drugs he had allowed into his life had clouded his judgement. He said he always knew he would die young but had loved the fame his music had brought him. It had been a blast, and he'd had a great time.

He didn't stay around for long; the session was fast and short. As a spirit, he said what he wanted to say quickly, then was gone.

Words of wisdom

Music is my religion, man.

Pursue what catches your heart, not what catches your eyes.

If you don't like the path you're walking on, start paving another one.

You define your own life.

Stay away from those people who try to disparage your ambitions.

How you love yourself is how you teach others to love.

Use boundaries at all times, in personal relationships as well, as people are often not who they say they are.

It's okay to live your life the way you want, but you don't always have to carry everyone. Life is not a free ride.

Katharine Hepburn

Born: 12 May 1907, Harford,
Connecticut, United States
Died: 29 June 2003, Fenwick, Connecticut,
United States – Parkinson's disease.
Astrological sign: Taurus
Day number 3: Builders of the world, highly creative,
have an eye for beauty, hard workers.

Katharine Hepburn was an indomitable, strong-spirited American actress and comedian who was loved by many, both women and men. Her career spanned six decades. Unfortunately, she had a health condition. Her illness, an essential tremor, gave her a quavering voice and trembling hands. She was extremely intelligent and achieved great success in her career. She won the most Academy Awards for Best Actress, winning four times, during her years in the golden age of Hollywood, and had a strong screen persona that matched her public image.

Katharine let people know she was not religious, she was in fact an atheist, and believed people should be kind to others. She was blessed to have not only great talent, but also beauty, strong independence and a big personality to go with it; she was very outspoken for a woman of her era.

She started with a very hard life and survived starvation during the Second World War, which contributed a lot to her health, fragility and wellbeing. Her sexuality was wildly discussed, and it was said she had lesbian relationships as well as relationships with men, loving everyone deeply. Her greatest love was Spencer Tracy, whom she met at Metro-Goldwyn-Mayer. Their alliance spanned twenty-six years.

Katharine changed the popular perceptions of women at the time, and in 1999 was named the greatest female star of classic

Hollywood cinema by the American Film Institute. Some of her films included *The Philadelphia Story, Guess Who's Coming to Dinner, On Golden Pond, The African Queen* and *The Lion in Winter.*

The séance: When Katharine came through, she said she was extremely curious about what we were doing and was happy to talk to us. Each time she spoke, I could feel her hesitate, as if she was thinking very deeply about what she wanted to say. She said she wanted to tell things her way.

The first thing she said was, she felt it was important to be independent and for women and men to have freedom in life, as she'd had. She said her life had been easy because her work was her passion. She loved what she did, because the study of people's characters as individuals was what good actors did, right down to knowing their tiniest details and habits. We got the impression she must have been a perfectionist in her work, and she was said to have dedicated a lot of time to her craft when she was acting. When playing a role, she lived the part.

When asked about the Second World War, she said the war had been terrible for humankind and very hard for her, but it had given her the values and strength in life to conquer anything she wanted, to appreciate everything that came her way and not to waste good opportunities. When asked about her love life, she talked about her great love, Spencer Tracy – her 'soulmate'. She said they'd had a very strong connection and he challenged her intellectually, which was refreshing. They were a legendary couple, she said with a laugh, although they had never married. Although Spencer claimed he was unhappy in his marriage, he stayed with his wife until he died. Katharine said his wife was at his side when he passed.

Words of wisdom

I'm a personality as well as an actress.

People have grown fond of me, like some old building.

I don't regret anything I've done, as long as I enjoyed it at the time.

It would be great if people could get to live suddenly as often as they die suddenly.

Love has nothing to do with what you're expecting to get, only with what you're expecting to give, which is everything.

Not everyone is lucky enough to understand how delicious it is to suffer.

I wear my sort of clothes to save me the trouble of deciding which clothes to wear.

Philip Seymour Hoffman

Born: 23 July 1967, Fairport, New York, United States
Died: 2 February 2014, West Village, New York, United States – acute mixed drug intoxication after more than two decades of sobriety.
Astrological sign: Leo
Day number 5: Quick thinkers, kind, charismatic, creative, very restless, have excellent communication skills, may be fickle.

Philip Seymour Hoffman was a talented American actor, well known for his supporting roles as eccentrics, underdogs, and misfits. He was also a producer and theatre director. His most famous role was his Academy Award-winning portrayal of Truman Capote in the 2005 movie, *Capote*. He also took the main role of Willy Loman in Arthur Miller's play, *Death of a Salesman*, a performance that earned him a Tony Award nomination.

Although a talented actor, he struggled with drug addiction for much of his younger years. He abstained for several years but unfortunately had a relapse and died two years later. He was found inside his New York City apartment with a needle stuck in his arm, dead from a possible heroin overdose. At the time of his death, he was filming *The Hunger Games: Mockingjay: Part 2*, which was released in 2015.

He acted in many films and theatrical productions, right up until his death, and was voted one of the fifty greatest actors of all time.

The séance: When Philip's spirit came through, it was with a lot of playfulness. He spoke fondly of how he loved to play all his characters with great authority, even down to the way they grunted, walked or slurred their words, which he conceded may have been annoying to those around him. He said he'd found it amusing to do this and was a lot of fun. It not only entertained his followers, he said, but himself as well. He loved to study the idiosyncrasies of the character he was portraying because it enabled him to find depth in the character.

He said that even though he didn't have much luck in controlling his own life, with his history of addictions, through his work he was able to break free of all restrictions and really get into the character's persona, forgetting who he was and letting go of any sadness.

Towards the end of the session, he spoke mostly about his children and family, and how important it was for him to have supportive people in the background who loved him, especially his children. It had meant a lot to him, even as a child, to have this strong foundation in his life.

He spoke about his personal life, and the love and joy his children had given him. He said he was sad to have passed so young, as he'd had projects on the boil, but he understood it was his time. He'd been fighting his own demons for so long, and it was like having a black cloud around his head, which was difficult to hide at times. He also said he'd had no intention of dying when he did, calling it a misalignment in his thoughtforms.

Words of wisdom

Stop searching for what you're searching for, as it's generally right in front of you.

Don't let people treat you like a cigarette; they'll only use you when they're bored and step on you when they're done. Be like drugs, let them die for you.

The film is made in the editing room.

The only true currency in this bankrupt world is what you share with someone else when you're uncool.

Creating something else is all about problem solving.

Was I happy? Or was I just not aware?

Success isn't what makes you happy. It really isn't. Success is doing what makes you happy, and doing good work, and hopefully having a fruitful life. If I've felt like I've done good work that makes me happy. The success part of it is all gravy.

BOB HOPE

Birthname: Lester Townes 'Bob' Hope
Born: 29 May 1903, in London,
England, United Kingdom
Died: 27 July 2003, in Los Angeles, California,
United States – pneumonia.
Astrological sign: Gemini
Day number 2: Peacemakers, intuitive, spiritual, sensitive,
may suffer from mood swings.

Everyone loves comedy. Bob Hope was an English-born American comedian, actor, producer and entertainer. After a brief career as a boxer in the 1910s, he moved into show business in the early 1920s, becoming a comedian, vaudevillian, actor, singer, dancer, and author. In his early performance career he was a busker. He was from the golden era of Hollywood.

His highly successful career spanned over eighty years, and he appeared in more than seventy short and feature films. He made a series of seven road musical comedies with Bing Crosby, whom he called 'The crooner'. It's said that in real life, the two men never got on. Besides smirking a lot, as if he was about to tell a joke, Bob loved nothing better than to wear a 'pinkie', the ring he considered a symbol of success.

He also hosted the celebrated Academy Awards nineteen times – more than any other host – and he was the author of fourteen books.

The séance: When Bob came through the medium, and the control asked who I was speaking to, the younger sitters in the group had no idea who he was. Bob, like many spirits who began to come through in some of the sessions, were famous icons from the golden years of Hollywood. The group often joked the energy was going through a different phase, as many old and famous spirits were beginning to come through, with Bob being one of them.

The reason I remembered him was because my father was a big fan back in the day and loved all Bob's work, especially his humour and wit. I don't know how many times I saw Dad watching Bob's old movies on TV and laughing with delight.

When Bob came through, he seemed to have a lot to say. The messages he gave to the sitters were quite political; he said he did not like the current president of the United States and that he, himself, was a Democrat.

Bob turned out to be a bit of a joker and tongue-in-cheek personality. When I channelled him, he began playing with some of the questions the group asked him, and, although in a deep trance state, I could hear some of them giggling and laughing. It was hard to take him seriously. It turned out he was into sports as well, and he spoke about golf.

He also spoke about his bad habit of sucking on big cigars. Bob's energy affected me at the time, because as he spoke through me to the group, I could sense a heaviness in the back of my throat, which made me stop talking and cough a couple of times. Even though Bob was a smoker, he lived to the age of one hundred, which puzzles me. He said he liked driving his Cadillac; it gave him a lot of pleasure and made him feel 'king of the road'. He mentioned his wife, who was religious, and how much he cared about her, but later research revealed he was a renowned womaniser.

Words of Wisdom

Don't worry about the rest of the gang, just do it.

Take time out from the crowd and do your own thing.

Make sure you do something different. Don't be like the rest of the herd. Surprise me.

Keep them guessing and show them how they don't know you.

Get some life skills by being a leader; let everyone one else guess what's going on.

Being independent or different can mean having life skills to take care of your physical needs, like playing golf, or paying bills, but it's also about being able to think for yourself and make the right choices that reflect your beliefs and desires.

Achieving independence can make a difference in how we feel and see ourselves in the world around us. Don't be afraid to step into the unknown and be a trailblazer, as people will be attracted to this.

Barry Humphries

Born: 17 February 1934, Melbourne, Victoria, Australia
Died: 22 April 2023, Sydney, New South Wales, Australia – complications after surgery.
Astrological sign: Aquarius
Day number 8: Good businesspeople, know how to make money, self-confident, need to be careful when selecting partners.

Barry Humphries AO CBE was a well-known and much-loved Australian comedian, actor, author, art curator and satirist. Based in London, he described himself as 'an ancient comic'. He was renowned for his work, which included writing and playing stage and television characters who were larger than life.

Dame Edna Everage was probably the most famous of his characters internationally. She was named after Humphries' first nanny. Dame Edna was originally conceived as the 'Moonee Ponds housewife' and launched in a sketch depicting the difficulties facing a Melbourne hostess in receiving foreign visitors. Barry made the character into a bourgeois Melbourne suburbs housewife. Edna was at times insulting and intrusive, but still likeable and sincere.

Over the years, he became extremely successful at portraying Dame Edna, and his acts translated well to overseas audiences. Some of his shows were *Housewife! Superstar!*, *Edna the Spectacle*, and *Dame Edna the Royal Tour*, bringing him international stardom. He toured with this character for many years on stage, in film, and on TV.

His other character, Sir Les Patterson, was based on a fictional character – a vulgar, drunken Australian politician.

Barry had four wives, and when he died, he was surrounded by his wife of forty years, Lizzie, and his beloved children.

The séance: Barry came into a meditation the day after he died and not in the usual séance structure, with the group energy. I'm still convinced he jumped the line and, as I'm sure he's as busy in spirit as he was on Earth, he had no intention of waiting until the séance was back on. Of course, I was overjoyed to work with him, alongside my main guide, who stepped in. I was surprised and saddened by Barry's death, so I just went with it, having a laugh to myself, thinking bless, this is happening to me, in my home office. I have always been a big fan, and it was good to hear his voice, as he told me he had arrived safely in the spirit world.

As I listened to him quietly, in a deep trance state, I felt him transfigure over my face and heard him say, very cheekily, 'Hello, possum, I'm happy to meet you.' (*Transfigure* is a spiritual term in mediumship that means to change the form or appearance of someone or something.) Then I heard a loud laugh. I can only imagine living with Barry would have meant living with a crowd; he had so many quirky characters.

Barry said he could only describe his life as extraordinary, with lots of ups and downs. He was delighted with his incredible success because it opened many doors that may not have happened otherwise. He said he had totally enjoyed the ride.

He said his work had been invaluable to him, as he loved throwing himself into different personalities; he said it was like therapy and very enjoyable. He also said it was very healing on so many levels, especially when dealing with life's frustrations, as performing helped him understand the personality of the person, which was something he played on. Exaggerating that was very funny for him, and he often heard the characters talking in his head.

As the session was coming to an end, I could feel his spirit becoming weaker. Then he quickly said he had loved his wives and his family, and talked about his 'lovely Lizzie', who he said was 'my girl'.

WORDS OF WISDOM

Don't be afraid to break the rules.

Always follow your passions. You can do anything once you make your mind up.

Be creative, as you have natural gifts and may be a natural performer or comedian.

Sometimes, by being different characters, we can express ourselves in better ways, as if we're standing outside of ourselves and having a laugh at the things that happen in our lives.

Expression is very important for all of us.

Change is a good thing. It always has a lot of energy coming to the surface, so the new you can emerge.

A reinvention or reset is good at different times in our lives as we work on ourselves.

Stop making excuses and stand up now for what is right for you, as the rest will follow. Big changes are on the horizon, and you are ready to fly.

Marc Hunter

Born: 7 September 1953, Taumarunui, New Zealand
Died: 17 July 1988, Berry, New South Wales, Australia – throat cancer.
Astrological sign: Virgo
Day number 7: Spiritual, need to listen to their own intuition, always looking for deeper meanings in life, hang onto things.

Marc Hunter was a pop singer, songwriter, record producer and the lead vocalist of Dragon, a band formed by his older brother, Todd. Marc was a big personality and was known to be recklessly outspoken and aggressive on stage, to the point where was fired by Todd, who ran the band. Marc later returned to the band but also maintained his solo career. In July 2008, Dragon was inducted into the ARIA Hall of Fame.

Marc and Todd grew up in a musical family in Taumarunui, New Zealand. Both pursued separate musical careers until Todd invited Marc to join his band in 1973. Marc was the focal point, and he possessed a striking stage presence with his androgynous good looks and imposing height (both he and Todd were well over 180 centimetres tall), which was accompanied by an utter fearlessness in front of hostile audiences.

The séance: Marc decided to make a visit a few years ago. After the séance, I found out that a friend of his was in the room – a woman who used to work with him in a recording studio. I didn't know any of this until the end of the session. At the same time, a producer and crew were there doing a radio segment for the ABC, called *Suburban Psychic on Earshot*, with David Rutledge, so I was a bit nervous before the session and kept wondering how it would go.

As I have explained, as the medium, I never have any idea who's going to come through on the night, so when the control asked who we were talking to, I was surprised. I was never a fan of Marc, nor did I know much about him. With hindsight, I believe he came through because his old friend was present that night, and he wanted to get a message of love across, as spirits do.

When Marc was speaking through me, I could feel his big energy running through my body. I could also hear the woman's voice asking him personal questions; she must have been shocked when he came through as well. The poor woman sounded distressed and was in tears most of the time. The things they discussed were personal.

Marc also spoke about how he loved singing and music. He said he was a restless soul, so music had been very healing for him. He also spoke about his wife and daughter, whom he loved very deeply. He said the cancer had been really hard for him, but he'd always made an effort to stay calm as he knew, deep down, it was his time. The trouble was, he said, he loved smoking cigarettes.

WORDS OF WISDOM

Never give up on your dreams.

Eat your cereal with a fork and do your homework in the dark.

I'm sick of being ashamed. I don't mind being dejected and rejected, but I'm not going to be ashamed about it.

Just look inside yourself and you'll see me waving up at you, naked, wearing only a cock ring.

They say I'm disturbed.

All the great themes have been used up and turned into theme parks.

Now I'm depressed. Now I feel like killing myself, but luckily I'm too depressed to bother.

Michael Jackson

Born: 29 August 1958, in Gary, Indiana, United States
Died: 25 June 2009, in Los Angeles, California, United States — cardiac arrest caused by acute propofol and benzodiazepine intoxication administered by his doctor, Conrad Murray.
Astrological sign: Very driven Virgo
Day number 2: Peacemakers, intuitive, spiritual, sensitive, may suffer from mood swings.

Michael Jackson was known as the King of Pop. He was an American singer, songwriter and dancer. He is regarded as one of the most significant cultural figures of the 20th century and one of the greatest entertainers. He was a popular figure in culture for over four decades. As a child, he made his professional debut in 1964 with his brothers in a group called the Jackson 5.

When he became a solo artist, he popularised complicated dance techniques such as the moonwalk, which he named. His incredible sound influenced artists across many genres, and he was regarded as a genius. Unfortunately, his life changed when he became a figure of controversy and speculation due to his changing appearance, relationships, behaviour and lifestyle. Allegations of child sexual abuse led to an international backlash against him after his death.

Listening to his music, you can feel the energy, which makes you feel alive, like turning on a lightbulb.

The séance: Tuning into Michael in the séance was very different from what I had imagined. I felt him to be a very gentle soul. He talked nonstop about his work and said he knew nothing except his music, writing, and singing. It was no wonder, he said, that he was completely devoted to his music and art. He loved making music and being creative; he said it was everything to him and really the only thing he knew.

He also came across as a very lost and small child, and talked slowly, as if being careful with his words. After a while he spoke about his family. In life, he was almost a recluse, as though trusting people may have been difficult for him. In society and the rest of the world, he was a misunderstood man socially, but an incredible artist who expressed himself though his music, dance and lyrics, always taking it further each time with his dedication to his craft.

Michael has come through a few times in the group, and each time he spoke about his beloved monkey, Bubbles. Michael said Bubbles was his greatest friend and had been a large part of his life for a while.

During most of the session, Michael spoke like a child and had everyone in hysterics with his way of seeing the world. It made us all aware that we had to be careful of the people we surround ourselves with. The control never asked about the allegations as the subject did not come up.

Words of wisdom

If you want to make the world a better place, take a look at yourself, then make the change.

I just wish I could understand my father.

I'm just like anyone.

The meaning of life is contained in every single moment of life.

I'm a black American. I am proud of my race.

My mother is wonderful.

I can accept failure. Everyone fails at something. But I can't accept not trying.

Janis Joplin

Born: 19 January 1943, Port Arthur, Texas, United States
Died: 4 October, 1970, Hollywood, California, United States – heroin overdose.
Astrological sign: Capricorn
Day number 1: Born leaders, independent, ambitious, hardworking, prefer to work on their own rather than with others, can be stubborn.

Janis Joplin was an American singer, songwriter and performer. She was one of the most iconic and successful female rock performers of her time, known for her raw performances and powerful mezzo-soprano vocal range. She also had electric stage energy when she performed her psychedelic rock, blues and soul music. She performed at Woodstock and played in several bands before going solo. *Rolling Stone* magazine ranked her number twenty-eight in its 2008 list of greatest singers of all time. She was known to have a quick wit and had an IQ of 165. It's also believed she had bipolar disorder, body dysmorphia and ADHD. It was also documented she had a dependency on drugs and alcohol. She often played at the same venues as Jimmy Hendrix.

The séance: Speaking to Janis was quite an experience. A rebellious spirit, she was very chatty and talked quite quickly, as if she had a lot to say. She said with every concert and performance, she had given everything she could and totally emerged herself in each performance as if it was her last. She loved to perform, she said, but had little control over her dependency on drugs and drink; she felt they gave her an edge when it came to her performances.

When we asked Janis about her love life, she said she had loved many, and had loved to have passion, drugs and sex in her life. She said her life had been very fast and it was difficult for her to keep control of her life at times, and she knew she hadn't looked after herself; she'd often felt her life was out of control. She had also worried about her vocal cords, feeling the strain of having to belt out the notes. Her whole life had been about music, and she had spent most of her time with many tunes in her head.

She kept repeating that she wished she'd had more time and more control of her life, which seemed to have spun so very quickly. She said she'd liked to make her own destiny, didn't like people telling her what to do and had never relied on anyone. She had done it all her way because life was meant to be that way.

Words of wisdom

Do things your own way. Don't compromise yourself.

I always wanted to be an artist, whatever that was, like other hicks want to be stewardesses.

Texas is okay if you want to settle down and do your own thing quietly, but it's not for outrageous people, and I was always outrageous.

When you think you have everything going okay, that's when it's dangerous.

There isn't going to be any turning point.

Always be free, it's worth it. Freedom is everything to me.

Singing, it's like, it's like loving somebody; it's a supreme emotional and physical experience.

Jack Kerouac

Birthname: Jean-Louis Lebris de Kérouac
Born: 12 March 1922, Lowell, Massachusetts, United States
Died: 21 October 1969, St Petersburg, Florida, United States – abdominal haemorrhage.
Astrological sign: Pisces
Day number 3: Builders of the world, highly creative, have an eye for beauty, hard workers.

Jack Kerouac, of French-Canadian ancestry, came from a family of potato farmers. Well known as an American novelist and poet, he is recognised as a pioneer of the Beat Generation, which paved the way for the hippie movement in the 1960s, by challenging the widely held beliefs of the time.

His works covered such topics as Catholic spirituality, jazz, promiscuity, Buddhism, drugs, poverty and travel. He was an underground celebrity of the hippy movement and led a very unconventional life. After his death at the age of forty-seven, he became famous, and since then his literacy prestige has grown, with several previously unknown works being published. I first became interested in his work as a young woman, while living in Norway and travelling around the world.

The séance: When Jack came through in the séance, most people didn't know of him, but they loved what he had to say. At first, he was slow to speak, and even when prompted by the control, he still did not have a lot to say. He was quite reluctant to say much at all and was difficult to talk to, which was possibly what he was like in life. I had the sense, though, perhaps he hadn't come through for the sitters in the room, but to give me a private message, letting me know he was in the background. He encouraged all of us in the world to keep writing our own stories, as sometimes confessions can take a load off, and can be good to give one insight.

If a spirit has been a bad communicator on Earth, they will be the same in the spirit world. I sensed Jack's spirit was very restless. He spoke about how he had wasted a lot of his time with his addictions, trying to find himself. He had found a way to express himself, not by talking but by writing. I found his works wonderful, and they enabled me to reflect on what Jack was discovering about himself and the world around him as he wrote them.

We are all travellers in life, and the message from Jack was to keep on travelling and exploring everything around us.

Words of wisdom

I had nothing to offer anybody, except there are many different roads to choose from.

If you have a good story, tell it.

Stories take you to great beauty, language, freedom and imagination to get your point across.

I'm constantly seeing new things in the world. My eyes are always open, as I don't like the mundane.

Always look for new ideas; they're often better than the old, which can take you around in circles, around and around, getting you nowhere.

Everyone has a story or two when you take the time to sit down and listen.

Language is a gift from the gods.

VAL KILMER

Born: 31 December 1959, Los Angeles, California, United States
Died: 1 April 2025, in Los Angeles, California, United States – throat cancer.
Astrological sign: Capricorn
Day number 4: Down to earth, have difficulty making decisions, honest and trustworthy.

Val Kilmer was an iconic, brilliant and charismatic American actor. At seventeen, he was the youngest person to be accepted into the Drama Division at The Juilliard School. He worked on stage, and later in films. As a method actor, he threw himself into his roles, fully living the characters. He also starred on Broadway and had great success in several other projects.

He started his film career in 1984, and appeared in *Tombstone*, *Batman*, *Willow*, *Thunder Heart*, to name a few. He played an incredible and unforgettable role in *The Doors*, which he took very seriously, immersing himself in the part and even singing the lyrics too. The band said they could not, at times, tell the difference between him and Jim Morrison, the original singer of The Doors. His final film was *Top Gun: Maverick*, in 2022, reprising his role from the original film. With his roles, Val was not a fan of live auditions but preferred to send videotape footage instead.

He was first diagnosed with throat cancer in 2015 and lost the power of speech when he underwent a tracheal procedure that damaged his vocal cords. He also underwent chemotherapy and had two tracheotomies, later dying of pneumonia in 2025.

He told *The New York Times* in 2020 that the vocal training he learned at Juilliard in his younger years helped him communicate when the throat cancer affected his speech.

He married only once, but dated many famous women, including Cher, Cindy Crawford, Angelina Jolie and Daryl Hannah. Cher was a big influence in his life and helped him throughout his illness. There is a Val Kilmer museum today, which displays his art.

The séance: Talking to Val Kilmer in the séance was easy to do, as his soul was very spiritual. He came across as an articulate, creative artist, a deep thinker who thought about the world a lot and his role in it. He was a gentle soul who did not like any wars and saw himself as an artist who loved nature. He had been interested in spirituality since he was young, and his strong Christian values were formed at an early age. He said the gift of prayer was an incredible thing and a miracle and was the way he had been raised.

When asked about his illness, he said he had learned to live with it. Although he couldn't speak, he never lost his voice because he'd found other ways of expressing himself, for example, through writing, painting and photography.

He said when his voice was taken away, although frustrating at times, he'd taken everything in his stride and made the most of his other gifts. He said that as a non-speaker, towards the end of his life he had become a great observer of life, and said he loved and appreciated nature, and the people in his life, so much. Real love and companionship with people on his level had been very important to him.

Val also said that, in general, his life had been incredible. He was very grateful and couldn't believe how much he'd been able to do. Every single experience in his life had been special, which he greatly appreciated, and his faith and belief in magic had always helped him. He saw himself as a free spirit, and he'd had so many magical moments and memories. After saying all this, he then left.

Once the séance was over and I came back into my body, we all sat around and said what a beautiful, strong soul Val Kilmer was.

Words of Wisdom

I think death is just a transition to another state of consciousness.

Life is precious, and when someone dies it's an opportunity to understand how precious it is. My brother drowned when I was seventeen. He was fifteen. I think I grew from that. My father didn't. It really crushed him.

I'm a character actor, but I look like a leading man.

I don't think my life is a cliché, but I'm a cliché eccentric.

You are my sun, my moon, my starlit sky. Without you I dwell in darkness.

My perception is that I've never done anything but work really hard.

Youth is seen in everything. You don't know anything when you're young. It's great being older, just having a more balanced perspective. I wake up and realise that what seemed to be important last year no longer is. I'm increasingly grateful for every day.

Vivien Leigh

Born: 5 November 1913, Darjeeling, India
Died: 8 July 1967, London, England, United Kingdom – tuberculosis.
Astrological sign: Scorpio
Day number 5: Quick thinkers, kind, charismatic, creative, very restless, have excellent communication skills, may be fickle.

After completing her drama-school education, Vivien Leigh became a renowned British stage and film actress who was always very passionate about her work. She was known to be a perfectionist and took her acting career very seriously. Vivien Leigh also lived with bipolar disorder, which contributed to the periods of depression she experienced throughout her life. It was challenging to manage and caused significant strain for her and those close to her. She later acknowledged that the severity of her episodes sometimes made it difficult for her to work. Later she developed tuberculosis, which some say was a result of her heavy smoking, as she consumed four packets a day.

In her golden years, she won two well-deserved Academy Awards. She was best known in the epic film *Gone with the Wind*, and the Tennessee Williams play and film *A Streetcar Named Desire*, plus many more creative projects.

She was married to the famous British actor, Lawrence Olivier, who has himself stated his relationship with her was love. Her work was her passion and she gave it everything.

The séance: When Vivien came through in the séance, she spoke very slowly and carefully with a British accent, well pronounced. She told us that acting had been her greatest passion. She also said how important it was to be disciplined to reach your personal and creative goals, adding she had always thrown herself into her craft.

She said her craft was everything, and she'd been thrilled it took her to such great heights and enabled her to become a star.

Vivien came across as very determined, a perfectionist with a strong spirit energy, and I could imagine channelling her, as she was very articulate in the way she spoke through me. I sensed that when she'd been alive, she wouldn't have let anything stop her from what she wanted to achieve with her work and her life—even though her body seemed very small and fragile—because she seemed so determined in her beliefs.

Then she spoke of her illness, and how she'd felt she had lost control of her life and wasn't able to be the person she'd wanted to be. She said it had been a painful experience.

On a personal level, Vivien was one of my all-time favourites. I had also been an actor for many years and have always admired her work and her acting skills, so it was a thrill when she managed to come through for all of us.

WORDS OF WISDOM

If you want to be a star, learn to be authentic first, and you will do well.

Oh Lord, I'm so grateful I'm still loved.

I've always been mad about cats.

Life is too short to work so hard.

I adore dancing.

Sometimes I dread the truth of the lines I say.

I'm not a film star; I am an actress.

John Lennon

Born: 9 October 1940, Liverpool,
England, United Kingdom
Died: 8 December 1980, New York City,
United States – gunshot wound.
Astrological sign: Libra
Day number 9: Imaginative, passionate, creative, have strong spiritual beliefs, like to run their own show, have trouble trusting, need to let go of things that no longer serve them.

John Lennon was an English singer, songwriter, musician and political activist from Liverpool, England. He struggled with dyslexia most of his life and was raised by his Aunt Mimi after his parents died. While attending high school, he excelled at art and music.

In the 1960s, he was co-founder of the world-renowned band, The Beatles, which achieved worldwide fame. In the band, he played guitar, keyboards and harmonica and sang. The group's genres were rock, pop, and experimental music. Lennon's songwriting partnership with Paul McCartney, remains the most successful in history. Some of the songs John wrote were 'I Want to Hold Your Hand', 'Help', 'Strawberry Fields', 'I Am the Walrus' and 'All You Need Is Love'.

After Brian Epstein's death in 1967, everything changed. Tensions grew from the bandmates' resentment of McCartney's domineering role, John's heroin use and his relationship with Yoko Ono, Harrison's prolific songwriting, and the later turmoil surrounding Apple Corps. The band members grew apart. Just before The Beatles disbanded, John formed another band with his second wife, Japanese artist Yoko Ono, and later became a solo artist.

John won many awards, and *Rolling Stone* magazine ranked him the fifth-greatest singer and thirty-eighth greatest artist of all time. In 1997, he was inducted into the Songwriters Hall of Fame.

In 1975, John stepped away from the music industry to raise his infant son. Five years later, he was murdered outside his Manhattan apartment building by a man who had been stalking him.

The séance: Tuning into John was a very funny and rowdy experience for the group. I had crossed paths with him before in other séances, with other mediums, so he was not a stranger, and I knew what to expect. My fond description of him is of a loud, obnoxious, bossy man who had a lot to say, and it was all said with a very strong Liverpudlian accent. He loved joking and swearing, but not in a bad way, and was very entertaining. I could imagine him having been a leader in life. At every sitting I went to, as well as those I conducted myself, he was always the same – a real joker and funster, except where politics were involved; then the tone would change.

Everyone in the group looked up to him, and he demanded all our attention in such a funny way with his brilliant wit and backhanded comments. The atmosphere in the séance room was brilliant. John's energy made everyone laugh and comment, and it was hard for the main sitter to control the group. As the medium, I found it hard to concentrate. In fact, I couldn't believe my ears at some of the things he said, but, in a trance state, I listened and repeated every word.

When asked about his greatest love, he said it had been his children, and he was chuffed at being a father. His fame had surprised him. He said that although he had reached the highest peaks, he'd been happier just doing his own thing. Music had always been in his head, even at a young age. One of his greatest songs was generally considered to be 'Imagine', but he said he couldn't decide if it was the best. He also said he loved working with his 'missus' and fellow artist, Yoko, as they were on the same page. One thing that stood out to me was, when he said he liked to see himself as a type of rebel.

Because I've chatted with John a few times over the years in other séances and have listened to him speak through other mediums in different groups, I found him easy to talk to. The dialogue was always the same – very direct and funny. When he wasn't talking about world peace, John offered different people advice if they were musicians.

I think of John as a brilliant yet complicated artist, with no airs and a lot to say.

Words of wisdom

A dream you dream alone is only a dream. A dream you dream together is reality.

Part of me suspects that I'm a loser and the other part of me thinks I'm God Almighty.

The only way to deal with critics is to go over their heads directly to the public.

God is a concept by which we measure our pain.

I've always been politically minded and against the status quo.

I was a working-class macho guy who was used to being served, and Yoko didn't buy that.

The Beatles' music died then, as musicians. That's why we never improved as musicians; we killed ourselves to make it. And that was the end of it.

Little Richard

Birthname:	Richard Wayne Penniman
Born:	5 December 1932, Macon, Georgia, United States
Died:	9 May 2020, Tullahoma, Tennessee, United Sates – bone cancer.
Astrological sign:	Sagittarius
Day number 5:	Quick thinkers, kind, charismatic, creative, very restless, have excellent communication skills, may be fickle.

Little Richard was an American singer, pianist and songwriter. He lived with disability his whole life, including an enlarged head and one leg and arm that were shorter than the other. This did not stop him, though, and he was an incredibly influential figure in popular music and culture for seven decades. He first started singing at church when he was younger, where he learned his musical gifts. His musical genres were rock and roll, rhythm and blues, gospel and soul. His nicknames included The Innovator, The Originator, and The Architect of Rock and Roll.

His music was characterised by his frenetic piano playing, flamboyant personality, raspy vocals, innovative emotive vocalisations, up-tempo rhythmic music and soul and funk. He was awarded a Grammy Lifetime Achievement Award and was inducted into the Rock and Roll Hall of Fame. His electrifying 1950s hits, 'Tutti Frutti' and 'Long Tall Sally', along with his flamboyant stage presence, influenced legions of performers.

The Beatles opened for Little Richard in some venues, and he advised them on how to perform his songs. His music was honoured by many institutions, and broke the colour lines, drawing black and white people together despite attempts to sustain segregation.

The séance: When Little Richard came through the medium and told the control who he was, he laughed loudly, whooped hello. The group felt his whirlwind of energy as he yelled and jumped around the room. He said, happily, he'd always had lots of energy as his soul was full. He went on to tell us he was born to sing, loved nothing better than to show off and have a good time because it was healing and made people laugh.

It was no wonder people called him 'The wild man of rock and roll'; the energy in the room was full on. Everyone was in stitches as he was so entertaining as he bounced energetically around the room.

When he spoke, he was full of enthusiasm, and he laughed a lot, showing everyone in the room his flamboyant personality. In real life, he identified as both a woman and a man, and it's no wonder he was known as the king *and* queen of rock and roll. His queerness is what made him a dynamic performer.

When asked, he said his influence had been massive while he was alive and he kept saying that he'd been a real performer. He'd loved to dress up and play the part because he knew the effect it had on people. He also told everyone in the group he loved women, and liked to do things with his hair, paint his face and wear lashes; he said when it was his time to come back, it would be as a woman. This made some people giggle. He also said he had lots of children around, but this is disputable, as we only know of his adopted son.

After the séance, the sitters were jumping out of their seats. We all had the feeling that Little Richard really knew how to make a statement and was a man with a message before his time.

Words of Wisdom

People who are different have, since the beginning of time, all been kicked and abused.

You gotta honour yourself, live the life you want and not be told how to do it.

Elvis may be the king of rock and roll, but I am the queen.

Greed has taken the whole universe, and nobody is worried about their soul.

God is omnipotent, He is omniscient and ever-present.

People called rock and roll 'African music'. They called it 'voodoo music'. They said it would drive the kids insane. They said it was just a flash in the pan, the same thing they used to say about hip-hop.

I think God made women to be strong and not to be trampled under the feet of men. I've always felt this way, because my mother was a very strong woman, without a husband.

Christine McVie

Born: 12 July 1943, Bough, England, United Kingdom
Died: 30 November 2022, London, England, United Kingdom – cancer and ischemic stroke.
Astrological sign: Cancer
Day number 3: Builders of the world, highly creative, have an eye for beauty, hard workers.

Christine was a musician and a singer. She came from a musical background. She was introduced to the piano at the age of four, studied music at eleven, and went on to become an iconic singer, keyboardist, and songwriter with the rock band Fleetwood Mac after she married John McVie, the band's bassist. It was later said she was the glue that kept the band together, even though the couple later divorced. Before her marriage, she was a talent in her own right. She played in various bands and worked with Fleetwood Mac as a session musician before joining two years later, performing lead vocals and remaining with the band through many changes.

She was inducted into the Rock & Roll Hall of Fame and received the Brit Award for Outstanding Contribution to Music in 1998, besides other achievements. She will always be remembered as being 'The best musician anyone could have in their band and the best friend anyone could have in their life'. Stevie Nicks said McVie had been her 'best friend in the whole wide world'.

The séance: When Christine came through in the séance, she had a very likeable, sweet, warm, articulate and welcoming energy and was easy to talk to. As the medium, I felt like I was talking to an old friend, as her spirit was so lovely. She came across as very personable. She spoke about her love of music, her great knowledge of her instruments, and how her life was built on this platform; it was something she'd known and been sure of her whole life. She'd loved to work with other musicians and enjoyed music on so many levels.

Christine said it had been a good way to communicate and express herself, as often art imitates real life. By the way she spoke through the medium, her tone was that of someone who had been very practical when she was in the living, and down to earth in the way she saw the world. She had been a hard worker, someone who functioned at a high level, always busy and curious to learn things. She said she'd loved meeting other artists, watching them work and being in the energy of their magic and creative flow. When the control asked her about her life, she said she'd loved nature and all it had to offer; it gave her comfort and peace, with the stillness it had to offer, and it had had a calming effect on her at certain times in her life.

As I sat with Christine's energy and channelled her into the séance, I saw symbols of music notes all around her. When I discussed this with the group later, we agreed it was no surprise since Christine had worked with music her whole life; it had been an integral part of her journey. All the sitters were in awe of her. She came across as very humble, and it was obvious she'd owned her creativity and had been happy to grow and explore more.

She said her death had been sudden, but she wasn't surprised when she saw herself in the spirit world, which she described as colourful and another adventure. She believed she had lived a full life.

WORDS OF WISDOM

When you work hard, the rest is easy. Go with the flow, and the highs and lows.

Believe in the old saying, 'When one door closes, another door will open.'

Don't get stuck in the mundane, it kills the spirit.

Watch for universal signs, as they are never wrong.

Know that being real is good, as you know your stuff, you are loved, so be honest.

It's now time to take action and believe you are the director and maker of your own reality. Nobody else can do this for you.

Always know when it's finished. When you know it's all over, it's time to move on.

Work hard, know your stuff and the rest will follow.

JAYNE MANSFIELD

Birthname: Vera Jayne Palmer
Born: 19 April 1933, in Pennsylvania, United States
Died: 29 June 1967, in New Orleans, United States – tragically, from injuries sustained in a car crash that also involved three other passengers.
Astrological sign: Aries
Day number 1: Born leaders, independent, ambitious, hardworking, prefer to work on their own rather than with others, can be stubborn.

As a young girl, Jayne Mansfield was determined to be a Hollywood star. She was very musical, studied ballroom dancing, played the violin and piano and took viola lessons. She later trained as an actor and entered beauty contests. She was also very intelligent, with a high IQ and spoke several languages; she was very different from her on-stage persona.

Jayne was also a major Hollywood sex symbol of the 1950s, a *Playboy* playmate and was known as a successful Broadway actress. Although her film career was short lived, she had several box-office successes, winning a Theatre World Award and a Golden Globe Award, and becoming known as 'Hollywood's smartest dumb blond'. She was also known for her wardrobe malfunctions. She was a big-busted blond bombshell, nightclub entertainer, singer, movie actress, and theatre and television star.

Her home was known as the Pink Palace, and she drove a pink Cadillac. She was known for her numerous publicity stunts and open public life.

The séance: As soon as Jayne spoke to the control through the medium, she was full of energy. She was very direct, passionate, full of life and was excited when she spoke happily about her work. She said she'd loved what she did and nothing would have stopped her doing it. She said she was nothing like the 'dumb blond' Hollywood knew her as.

When asked about her death, she said she was sad, as she'd had still had so much to do at the time. Her career had been on the rise, and she didn't like the way her life had ended. She also said she missed her man and her children. She went on to say that she had always been 'a woman on in mission'.

In life, she was definitely a person who knew what she wanted and went for it. As I channelled her, I had the feeling she would have given anything a go and hadn't been a soul who'd sat back and done nothing or waited for things to come to her. She came across as the sort of person who gave one hundred percent to everything she did. Besides 'wearing the pants' in her relationships, she'd had a very quick brain. She said she'd been a very loving person, had liked being single, and had loved with a passion. She repeated that her children were very important to her; they were everything to her, and she could never imagine having lived her life without them.

WORDS OF WISDOM

Give yourself the time to do everything you want and need.

If you have something to say, say it. Don't let others speak on your behalf.

If you've been feeling stuck, stop and just do what it is you need to do. Stop trying to please others, because at the end of the day this is your life, so make the best of it.

If you're having family or relationship problems, make peace, if possible. Be courageous and be the better person. Step forward, offer your love with an open heart and don't be afraid to be compassionate. If this doesn't work, cut the toxic ties and move on.

Life is too short to be stuck in these tricky situations that keep going around and around. They're timewasters.

I like being a pin-up girl, there's nothing wrong with that.

I want to earn my own way. I like having nice things, but I've never accepted anything I haven't earned.

I hope that I've given happiness to others, I hope I have given children to the world and that I have made some kind of a mark for myself here.

JIM MORRISON

Born: 8 December 1943, Melbourne, Florida, United States
Died: 3 July, Paris, France – heart failure.
Astrological sign: Sagittarius
Day number 8: Good businesspeople, know how to make money, self-confident, need to be careful when selecting partners.

Jim Morrison was a well-known and charismatic frontman, songwriter, poet and primary vocalist for the American rock band, The Doors. His death helped to set his image as a rockstar and sex symbol.

Some of his iconic songs are 'Riders on the Storm', 'Light My Fire' and 'People Are Strange'. In his younger days, he witnessed a road crash in which a Native American man was killed. Later in life, he said he sometimes felt the man's spirit enter him onstage, and he would channel that energy, dance, and say he was a shaman.

Also known as the Lizard King, Jim was a poet; he developed his talents as a performer by reciting poetry at the local Beaux Arts coffeehouse. During a 1969 concert in Miami, while doing his usual theatrics on stage, he exposed himself and was later charged with indecent exposure and profanity. He also developed an alcohol dependency, which at times affected his performance on stage.

After Jim's death, the band released the poetry he had recorded before his death on an album called *An American Prayer*. His life was made into a movie by Oliver Stone, called *The Doors*, and Val Kilmer was rewarded by the masses for his brilliant performance, even using his own singing voice.

The séance: When I called Jim into my channelled session and not into the séance, I could feel a whimsical, restless energy float into my body. I felt a natural high, which made me think he'd been a very spiritual person, and perhaps a dreamer in his short time on Earth. Before the session, his energy was present with me for days, so I knew he wanted to come through. He ended up staying for days after that; I heard his music in my head, playing over and over, which made me feel as if he wanted to be in the book and work with me.

He told me he was a curious, creative soul who wanted to try everything, above and beyond, and push the boundaries as far as possible. Not only with his tribe and his people, but with the whole community, with people from all walks of life, to make the statement that he could bend the rules.

He also spoke about love, and how important it had been for him to have a soulmate. He said he'd loved his long-time girlfriend, even though he slept with and experimented with many other women, but he couldn't help her with her addictions because he was experimenting heavily himself. He had struggled with all the attention from fans and was desperate for privacy.

Before he left, he said he was sad because he'd had so much more to give, but the next time he wouldn't harm himself as he had in this life, which was way too short for his liking.

Words of wisdom

Reset, move forward, explore.

Be free to explore all possibilities in life and don't restrict yourself or conform to a boring, mundane lifestyle.

Whatever talent you have, explore and play with it. You'll be amazed once you begin this journey, as your life will be like a resurrection. That's what I did.

I like people who shake other people up and make them feel uncomfortable.

The most loving parents and relatives commit murder with smiles on their faces.

There are things known and things unknown, and in between there are doors.

Love cannot save you from your fate.

Bert Newton

Birthname: Albert Watson Newton
Born: 23 July 1938, Fitzroy, Victoria, Australia
Died: 30 October 2021, Prahran, Victoria, Australia – complications related to ongoing health issues.
Astrological sign: Cancer
Day number 5: Quick thinkers, kind, charismatic, creative, very restless, have excellent communication skills, may be fickle.

Bert Newton AM MBE was a well-known and loved Australian media personality and comedian. He was inducted into the Logie Hall of Fame, a quadruple Gold Logie winner and an award-winning entertainer and radio personality. In Australia, he hosted the Logie Awards on seventeen occasions. He was at one time Graham Kennedy's TV sidekick, and worked with Don Lane as well as his wife, the singer Patti Newton.

Besides working in TV shows as a comedian and compere, his career started in radio broadcasting, primarily as an announcer, before becoming a star and fixture on Australian TV. He was considered an icon in his day and went on to become one of the longest-serving television performers in the world. While working in theatre as an actor, his appearances included *The Wizard of Oz*, *Beauty and the Beast*, *The Producers*, *The Sound of Music*, *The Rocky Horror Show*, *Grease the Musical*, and *Wicked*, which toured overseas.

When he died, Bert was given a State funeral in his hometown of Melbourne. He was a much-loved Australian legend, icon and entertainer.

The séance: Not long after Bert died, he came into the séance. We were all surprised as he came straight in when I went under. He spoke very clearly and wanted everyone to know he was doing okay, had survived his death, was no longer sick and suffering from diabetes and heart problems, was young again, with no pain and living happily in the spirit world. He said his spirit was full of energy again. He said he hadn't liked being sick, as he'd always felt he had so much to do, but he'd known he was running out of time because he got tired and could feel all his vital energy leaving him.

When the control asked him about his family, he talked mostly about his wife, Patti, whom he loved dearly. He said she was an amazing entertainer and, without a doubt, his partner in crime and the love of his life. She'd always been there by his side and supported him. He said he tried to contact her through dreams and wanted her to always have the best.

He also spoke about his love for his kids, and the constant highs and lows that go with most families. In fact, family meant a lot. He loved all his family but also loved his role in show business as a comedian, and entertaining had been his passion.

He said he was surprised to be with us as he didn't really believe in 'spooky stuff' and went on to tell us that his friend Don Lane was with him, who he remembered speaking very fondly of Doris Stokes, the famous medium from England, when she did a tour.

The night after Bert came through, a documentary was on television, with Bert, Don Lane and Graham Kennedy. It was ironic, and I believe this was Bert's way of saying a last hello and that our meeting had been authentic. This has happened to me with many of my channelled guests. I suppose it's spirit's way of confirming the authenticity of all the information I've received in all the work I've been doing in séances over the years.

Words of Wisdom

Go for everything that comes your way. It's far better when it comes to you.

Always have strong bonds with your partner, friends and loved ones. It's so important to have that strong foundation in life.

Always be generous with yourself and others.

If you have a strong talent and are eager to learn, learn as much as you can. The biggest secret is to have a go, give it your best shot and don't take no as an answer.

Life will not serve you well if you're content to just sit on the side lines.

The secret to life is to be kind and generous to everyone around you and to have an interest in learning and growing from these experiences.

Too many of us think we know it all and don't like to share. When you think or behave in this way, life becomes lonely and hard, and the road will be difficult. Generosity of spirit can create modern-day miracles.

Dame Olivia Newton-John

Born: 26 September 1948, Cambridge, England, United Kingdom
Died: 8 August 2022, Santa Ynez, California, United States – breast cancer.
Astrological sign: Libra
Day number 8: Good businesspeople, know how to make money, self-confident, need to be careful when selecting partners.

Olivia Newton-John was a well-loved British-born Australian singer, activist, philanthropist and actress, with over one hundred million records sold; she was the best-selling music artist of all time. The highest-ranking female Australian recording artist of all time, she was also a four-time Grammy Award winner whose music career included hits such as 'You're the One That I Want', 'Hopelessly Devoted to You' and 'Xanadu'. She will also be remembered for her role in the popular movie and musical, *Grease*.

In 2022, Olivia died of cancer, which she had three times and which she battled bravely for many years. She sponsored and advocated for breast cancer research. In addition, she was an activist in environmental and animal-rights causes. She had one daughter, Chloe, who has followed in her footsteps with her creativity.

The séance: When Olivia's delightful energy entered the room, her soft spirit radiated warmth and kindness, touching everyone. She spoke very gently, like a young girl, saying she missed her beloved daughter and her wonderful husband, John, who was not only her great love but a good friend to her, and had supported everything she believed in.

When asked questions by the control, Olivia talked about her cancer research, which had been a big part of her life. She claimed that through her research into alternative medicine, she had found a way to live a better life, and it had helped her live longer with her cancer, which she battled for many years. She also went on to say medicinal cannabis was great for cancer and dementia and had supported this for others through her humanitarian efforts. Her wish was for more people in the world, who were suffering, to be able to use medicinal cannabis, as it had helped her in so many ways. She also believed in whole foods and suggested we eat honey each day for its medicinal qualities. Before she left, she said goodbye and thanked us for talking with her.

Words of wisdom

Memories are always inside you. You can take them anywhere, always.

I love life and nothing intimidates me anymore.

I don't know what my path is yet.

Family, nature and health all go together.

You never know what the future holds, so I'm just enjoying being happy, healthy and having my wonderful husband by my side.

To be loved is the most basic of human needs. Like a flower, it waters the human soul. But to love is a true blessing.

There's a balance in my life. There's reality and there's the part that looks really glamorous, but we're all just people in the end.

Sinead O'Connor

Born: 8 December 1966, Dublin, Ireland
Died: 26 July 2023, Herne Hill, London, United Kingdom – complications of chronic obstructive pulmonary disease, asthma, and a respiratory infection.
Astrological sign: Sagittarius
Day number 8: Good businesspeople, know how to make money, self-confident, need to be careful when selecting partners.

Sinead O'Connor will always be remembered as a gifted talent with an incredible, unique voice that moved so many people. A Grammy Award winner, in the music industry, Sinead was considered an exceptional singer, songwriter and activist. Her album, *The Lion and the Cobra*, achieved international chart success. Her next album, *I Do Not Want What I Haven't Got*, was her biggest commercial success, selling over seven million copies worldwide. The album's lead single, 'Nothing Compares 2U', written by Prince, was honoured as the top single of 1990 at the inaugural Billboard Music Awards.

Throughout her career, Sinead's songs were used for films and collaborations with other artists, and she appeared at fundraising concerts. An integral part of her work was the attention she gave to child abuse, human rights, racism and women's rights. She protested against the Catholic Church. She also tore up a photograph of Pope John Paul II in protest against abuse, which caused a lot of controversy. Not long after, she converted to Islam, changing her name and keeping it to the end of her life. In 2024, she was inducted into the Rock & Roll Hall of Fame. She loved her children, who meant a lot to her.

The séance: As I contacted the spirit of Sinead, I sensed a very dear, intelligent and restless soul. As she had always said, she was fearless, and it had always been her desire to commit herself to anything she believed in. Without a doubt, she was brave, courageous and always happy to say her piece. During the session she was often outspoken. She said throughout her life she had been a very strong-minded person and a free thinker, someone who had a lot to say, without 'bullshit'. She was also an activist and supported political causes on every level. Her fighting spirit would not let her get away with anything and others who crossed her path with their false narratives.

She also said she had lived with depression throughout her life. Towards the end of her life, she said very quietly, she had become very tired from terrible sadness and personal battles after the death of her beloved son, who had been missing before his body was found. He had committed suicide. At times it was like a black cloud over her head, she said, that swallowed her with the mere memory of him, which was so painful. As one could imagine, this is one of the most painful experiences any parent could go through. The utter loss and devastation had been something she could not come to terms with. She and her son had an incredible connection, and she believed they had been soulmates, so it was no surprise when she laughed and told us she had met up with him again in the spirit world.

Then Sinead spoke fondly of her many loves, her rocky life, and the music that flowed through her veins, which she loved with a passion. She said she had always felt it was important to express herself. She'd had plans to do more work but had felt for a while she was running out of time. She hadn't felt well for a long time, but was determined to continue with new work, as this was her passion and something that had always driven her. She said that sadness and disappointment in her life had taken its toll on her soul however, even though she fought to be an independent freethinker and straight talker. At the time of her death, she had been looking forward to her next creative journey.

After the session finished, the sitters and I felt the sadness in the room, but we all agreed that Sinead would never have lived her life any other way.

Words of wisdom

Don't be afraid to stand tall, speak your truth and live a life full of authenticity always.

I don't do anything in order to cause trouble. It just happens that what I do naturally causes trouble.

When I sing, it's the most solitary state: just me, and the microphone, and the holy spirit. It's not about notes or scales, it's all about emotion.

We know we will win. We have confidence in the victory of good over evil.

To say what you feel is to dig your own grave.

I seek no longer to be a famous person, and instead I wish to live a normal life.

LISA MARIE PRESLEY

Born: 1 February 1968, Memphis, Tennessee, United States
Died: 12 January 2023, Los Angeles, California, United States – complications from bariatric surgery.
Astrological sign: Capricorn
Day number 1: Born leaders, independent, ambitious, hardworking, prefer to work on their own rather than with others, can be stubborn.

Lisa Presley, the only daughter of Elvis and Priscilla Presley, was born nine months to the day after her parents' wedding. Like her father – the American actor, musician, and cultural icon who died when she was nine – Lisa became an accomplished singer and songwriter.

Besides being a former member of the Church of Scientology, Lisa had several marriages, the most famous being to Michael Jackson, whom she felt she had to save during a difficult time in his life. She was also married to the actor Nicolas Cage. She inherited the original mansion and grounds of Graceland, Elvis Presley's legacy, where her father and son are buried.

Lisa had a big life, with many ups and downs, especially in her relationships. Her sadness was at its greatest when she lost her son to suicide, which people say she never recovered from.

The séance: When I tuned into Lisa in the group, her energy spoke very passionately, giving the impression she liked to do things in her own way. She also came across as a straight shooter, somebody who just said it how it was. She seemed very strong, and spoke lovingly about her father, how he spoiled her and how she had lived a big life in such a small amount of time. Lisa also spoke about her divorce and her ex, Michael Lockwood, who she believed was always after money, which made her angry.

Lisa had been a real fighter, loved her kids, and made up her own mind about the way she would do things, she said. She also spoke of the sadness of losing her beloved son and described it as overwhelming, terrible and tragic, and something she was never able to get over. She was stuck on the idea that she had not been able to save him, and that in some way it was her fault. It was perhaps a theme she suffered a few times.

She said she was now happy and at peace with her father and son in spirit and felt relieved they were both doing so well. She also spoke of a pony she was fond of. She said her children were her greatest legacy, as family was everything.

Words of wisdom

I don't do yoga, I bite my nails, I smoke, I eat all the wrong foods, I don't exercise.

You're always learning, there's a lot of grey, don't take things for granted.

I was quite the spoilt brat.

Anybody in the spotlight can get lost in that if they're not careful.

I think having kids just makes you want to do things to help people.

If I'm alone too much in my life, and I'm not interested in doing that, it won't lead anywhere good, I'm sure. If I'm busy I tend to stay out of trouble. An idle mind is the devil's playground.

Music has always gotten me through life, particularly honest, real music.

Princess Margaret

Birthname: Margaret Rose Windsor
Born: 21 August 1930, Glamis Castle, Scotland, United Kingdom
Died: 9 February 2002, London, England, United Kingdom – stroke.
Astrological sign: Leo
Day number 3: Builders of the world, highly creative, have an eye for beauty, hard workers.

Princess Margaret was the second daughter of King George VI and Queen Elizabeth. She was often portrayed as a controversial member of the British royal family, a woman before her time. She received much negative publicity after her divorce because of her controversial lifestyle and the several men she was associated with. She had been a free-spirited, glamorous woman, and a humanitarian, aware of her station in life and what she was allowed and not allowed to do.

Her main interests were welfare charities, music, ballet and men. Her turbulent life took a toll on her health in her later years. A heavy smoker like her father, she had part of a lung removed, but continued drinking. Throughout her life, her private activities were the subject of great speculation by the media and royal watchers. Her favourite place was her house on the island of Mustique, where she entertained people from all walks of life. She will always be best known for her impeccable sense of style and sharp wit.

The séance: When Margaret came into the séance, she seemed lively, very smart, socially aware and extremely chatty, like a young girl. She talked non-stop about her life, like she was just chatting on a phone, and how in the end she had always got her own way. It was easy to see why she'd been considered a very glamourous woman, curious and a bit of a rebel. She came across as friendly and happy to make a visit.

She said she had loved the fashions of the day, and gatherings with good friends made her happy. She also said she'd been loyal to her sister and had always stood by her, no matter the consequences.

Margaret's spirit was keen to know what we were doing, but then later chatted about her mummy, the Queen Mother; the arts; her relationships; and the very restricted life she refused to live. She also asked one of the sitters for a scotch on the rocks, with four ice cubes, then giggled.

She told us she used to party hard at Kensington Palace and that she used to sneak different lovers in through the back entrance. She hated the way she'd been told by the Queen how to walk, talk and behave, so instead she became a rebel. She also said she knew she would always be in her sister Elizabeth's shadow, as Elizabeth was destined for the throne.

Nothing was said about her children or exes; the talk was mostly about life. She kept saying she never regretted anything, had enjoyed herself immensely, and her pet hate was being bored or spending time with boring people.

WORDS OF WISDOM

No matter what the odds, you can live your life your way.

The queen is the only person who can put on a tiara with one hand while walking down the stairs.

I have always had a dread of becoming a passenger in life.

My children are not royal; they just happen to have the queen as their aunt.

When my sister and I were growing up, she was made out to be the goody-goody one.

The best way to succeed in anything is not to care too much about it.

It's a unique struggle to carve out an identity when everyone else sees you as a secondary.

Queen Elizabeth II

Birthname: Elizabeth Alexandra Mary Windsor
Born: 21 April 1926, London, England, United Kingdom
Died: 8 September 2022, Balmoral Castle, Scotland, United Kingdom – peacefully.
Astrological sign: Taurus
Day number 3: Builders of the world, highly creative, have an eye for beauty, hard workers.

Elizabeth II was queen of the United Kingdom and other Commonwealth realms from 1952 until her death in 2022. She was the descendent of Queen Elizabeth I, who was known as 'The Virgin Queen' until her death in 1603. Elizabeth II was the longest reigning monarch in British history. She was queen regent of thirty-two sovereign states during her lifetime and the monarch of fifteen realms at her death.

The cause of death was put down as old age. Her son, Prince Charles, became heir apparent at the time of her death, and the King of England after her death in 2022. Her other children include Princess Anne, Prince Andrew and Prince Edward.

The séance: When Queen Elizabeth came into the séance through the medium, her accent was very proper, upper-class English, and she was very polite and stoic, not showing any emotion. As the medium channelling her, I had the sensation of wanting to sit up nice and straight when she was speaking through me.

She said that after passing into the spirit world, she was now with Phillip and her beloved sister. She said she was worried about Charles and how he would lead her country, as he had always had ideas that were not similar to her own. She spoke about how she wanted William, Charles's eldest son, to take over in the future, and that it was part of her contract with her son, and something she wanted for the royal monarchy.

As for Diana, her son's first wife, Elizabeth said Diana never really fitted in, unlike Camilla Parker-Bowles, his second wife, who never really went anywhere, made herself available always, and stayed in the background.

As for Diana's revelation that there had been 'three of us in this marriage', the Queen said there'd been nothing she could have done about this as Charles had always done what he wanted in that department. Even though she was aware of the intense speculation in the media about this, she said that Camilla would be a great influence, and she'd been fond of Camilla when she was alive. They had a lot in common, like country life, gardening, and horses, the Queen's great love.

The Queen spoke fondly of her Corgis, which she had bred for many years, and said they had been good company for her. As for her husband, Phillip, she forgave him for his cheating ways during periods of their marriage, and she was grateful he had given up his life to serve her and be a good ear to talk to. He had always been by her side, as was his duty.

WORDS OF WISDOM

With success, there is no single formula. Stick to what feels right for you and what is expected.

I have in sincerity pledged myself to your service, as so many of you are pledged to mine.

When life seems hard, the courageous do not lie down and accept defeat; instead, they are all the more determined to struggle for a better future.

Success is the sum of small efforts, repeated day in and day out.

There is no substitute for hard work.

Helen Reddy

Born: 25 October 1941, in Melbourne, Victoria, Australia
Died: 29 September 2020, in Los Angeles, California, United States – dementia and Addison's disease.
Astrological sign: Scorpio
Day number 7: Spiritual, need to listen to their own intuition, always look for deeper meanings in life, hang onto things.

Helen Reddy was an Australian-American singer, actress, author, feminist and activist, and also a TV host. She was born into a show-business family. Her father was a theatrical producer, and her mother was an actress, and she spent most of her childhood touring with the family's vaudeville act. Her famous hit, 'I Am Woman', became an iconic feminist song in the 1970s and was intended as a tribute to all women.

During the 1970s, Helen enjoyed international success, especially in the United States. For a short period of her life, she also practised as a clinical hypnotherapist and motivational speaker. Throughout her life she worked with many famous people on talk shows and was passionate about her work. She was most famously called 'The queen of housewife rock' by Alice Cooper.

The séance: When Helen came into the séance, she spoke very softy through the medium. It took a while for her to warm up, and through closed eyes while deep in trance, I could sense her energy looking around the room. When she finally began to speak, she said she'd always been very down to earth and had thought deeply about which way she wanted to go with her work. We all had the distinct impression she'd been a very strong character and a deep thinker while alive, and that she'd never given up, no matter how difficult her life was.

As she moved even closer, she opened up more, and very kindly encouraged us all to follow our dreams and never lose sight of what we want to accomplish. Her words were powerful. She said throughout her life she had learned to always persevere, to never have any regrets and just keep going, which was very encouraging to us all.

She said that, if anything, she'd given her life her best shot, no matter what the consequences were. She said she knew she was born to entertain.

Words of wisdom

If I have to, I can do anything. I am strong, I'm invincible, I am woman.

Follow whatever your soul is yearning for; it is the right path. Don't listen to what others say.

With your inner strength and determination, it's time to dig deep, let go of any fears that are not true and leap into the unknown to start your exciting journey.

Trust your intuition and inner whisperings to guide you. Great success is yours when you stick to this course and know yourself.

You're not going to find a man whose socks don't get dirty, or who doesn't snore.

Depression, as far as I'm concerned, is just a waste of time.

I think that two people who decide to live together in a marriage situation have an obligation to make the marriage work for them.

CHRISTOPHER REEVE

Born: 25 September 1952, New York City, United States
Died: 10 October 2004, Mount Kisco, New York, United States – cardiac arrest while being treated for an infection related to a pressure sore.
Astrological sign: Libra
Day number 7: Spiritual, need to listen to their own intuition, always looking for deeper meanings in life, hang onto things.

Christopher Reeve was an award-winning American actor, director, author and activist. He had a passion for acting from an early age and was best known for playing the role of the superhero in the movie *Superman* and its three sequels. It's said he played the role with both charisma and grace. In his thirty-four-year career, he did everything with great passion.

With his political beliefs, he did much work for the environment and human rights causes for artistic freedom of expression. After his accident, he also lobbied for spinal-cord injury research, including human embryonic stem-cell research, and for better insurance cover for people with disabilities.

The séance: When Christopher came into the séance, the first thing he said after his name was that he'd always believed in what we were doing, as he'd always known he was a spiritual person, here to do great things. He said he always saw what he described as 'the bigger picture' in everything. He also shared he loved his work, which was no surprise, and he was very driven and hardworking in everything he did.

When asked about playing Superman, he laughed and said he'd loved playing the hero, but helping humanity, in any way, had been his passion while on Earth. He was limited not only by his physical body but also time. He had tried to do as much as he could in the limited time he'd had. He said that for him, time was always the essence.

As Christopher spoke through the medium, he came across as a truly loving spirit, with a great intellect. He told us that even as a small child he knew he had much to do, and also before his accident. He said he was proud of having been a humanitarian. He believed the world could be a better place and spoke lovingly of his determination to do great things in the world with his fame, which he had used as a platform.

When we asked him about his family and children, he said he'd always had great love for those close to him, as it was a gift. Then he continued to talk about his work. His mission had been to help people in any way he could, even though he'd lived with the terrible hardship of his disability for a good period of his life. He told us he had never given up on life, no matter what had come his way.

There was not one person in the group who did not have a tear in their eye after hearing such beautiful messages from such a humble soul. Christopher was also funny, and told a few jokes, which made us love him even more. His spirit was very honourable and compassionate, and his thirst for knowledge was obvious. Before he went, he joked that he loved the fact he had no disabilities now he was in spirit.

WORDS OF WISDOM

Be a risk taker and always tackle your problems full on. Don't give up, ever.

Always do and think like a true humanitarian, which is part of your spiritual purpose. If we all did this, we would be living in a better world.

Respect the knowing you have in your gut and heart. It's real, and there to help and guide you.

Tithing is a good way to help people and the community, and a new way to meet like-minded people. Don't be afraid of losing anything, as it always comes back.

Please surround yourself with the right people. It's the only way to be successful and move ahead.

Don't give up or lose hope.

So many of our dreams seem improbable, and then, when we summon the will, they soon become inevitable.

Debbie Reynolds

Birthname: Mary Frances Reynolds
Born: 1 April 1932, El Paso, Texas, United States
Died: 28 December 2016, Los Angeles, California, United States –stroke.
Astrological sign: Capricorn
Day number 1: Born leaders, independent, ambitious, hardworking, prefer to work on their own rather than with others, can be stubborn.

Debbie Reynolds was a well-known American actress, singer and entrepreneur. She was a vivacious personality and knew just about everyone in Hollywood. She was good friends with Frank Sinatra in her early days, and had gone to the same church as Marilyn Monroe. Her faith had always helped her throughout her life. He acting career spanned over seventy years, and she performed on television, film and stage. One of her most famous songs was 'Singing in the Rain'. Two of her movies were *The Tender Trap* and *The Affairs of Dobie Gillis*.

Throughout her life, Debbie survived her fair share of scandals, especially when her good friend Elizabeth Taylor ran off with Debbie's husband at the time, the crooner Eddie Fisher. Debbie first met Eddie while entertaining American troops during the Korean War. They were married in 1955, and had two children, Carrie and Todd. For a time, Debbie and Eddie were known as America's sweethearts.

The couple was also good friends with Mike Todd and Elizabeth Taylor. Mike died in a plane crash, and being a good friend of both Mike and Elizabeth, Eddie went to comfort Elizabeth. He never came back to his wife. Instead, he and Elizabeth embarked on a romantic affair, and before too long, Eddie became Elizabeth's next husband. Debbie, forever the trooper, was left to raise their two children.

Elizabeth and Eddie's marriage didn't last, and years later, Debbie forgave her good friend, and things just carried on.

After the shock and sudden death of her famous daughter, Carrie Fisher, just one day before her own, Debbie's last words were that she wanted to be with her daughter; they were not only mother and daughter but also great friends. They were finally buried together.

The séance: When I tuned into Debbie's energy in the séance, I was surprised by how lovely and friendly she was. She had a huge energy and a great sense of humour. She complained, jokingly, about how two of the things she most regretted in her life were her choice in men and her bad smoking habit, which she developed for roles in her films. She said the smoking had just taken over.

As she chatted away, I had the impression she had seen it all throughout her life and just went with the punches. There had always been so much going on. She also said she loved her kids; they were her greatest gift. She said she had not been good at reading people and had often got into trouble for being so trusting.

When she spoke of her varied career, she said she'd loved what she did as it had kept her on the go; there was always something going on. She loved her success and having experienced so much in one lifetime.

Her saddest memory, she said, was when her husband betrayed her. It had been such a shock, but she'd learnt to let it go. She knew her good friend Elizabeth had been inconsolable after Mike's death. She also mentioned that she loved her daughter, Carrie, and that they'd been very close, but that their relationship had been difficult. Sometimes they never talked for long periods, and that was hard, she said, but she always knew that Carrie would come back again. When her daughter died, it was a turning point; her heart was broken, and it was too much for her. At the end of the session, Debbie said she was happy to pass as her daughter was waiting for her.

Words of Wisdom

Don't hold onto things. It gives you too many worries, wrinkles and pain.

If I had a crystal ball, I would not have done anything differently.

You grow from all your experiences.

Meeting so many interesting people throughout my life made me want to be a better person and go for what I really wanted with my own talents.

Hard work never hurt anybody. You are only as good as your last performance.

I wish I had listened to all the advice I got over the years with men. It would've been easier, to say the least.

You're only as old as you think you are. I've never believed in ageism, that's for the birds.

Never leave things until it's too late. Make the move and never give up on peace, no matter how difficult or lost the other person is.

You never stop loving anyone, ever.

Alan Rickman

Born: 21 February 1946, London, England, United Kingdom
Died: 14 January 2016, London, England, United Kingdom – pancreatic cancer.
Astrological sign: Aquarius
Day number 3: Builders of the world, highly creative, have an eye for beauty, hard workers.

Alan Rickman was a talented English actor and director. He was well known and respected for his craft. He had a deep, distinctive, languid voice and trained at the Royal Academy of Dramatic Art in London. He appeared on stage, TV and in films. He became a member of the Royal Shakespeare Company, performing in classical theatre productions. When he worked on Broadway, he was nominated for a Tony Award.

Alan is probably most well known and loved for his portrayal as Severus Snape in the *Harry Potter* movies. Most of the sitters knew him mainly for the mean character he played in the movies, but in the session, he came across as witty and a true gentleman. We didn't know what to expect and were pleasantly surprised his real character was so different from that of the villain, Severus Snape. He was such a gentle, lovely man that we decided he must have been stretched, and a really good actor, to have played the character so well.

In life, Alan got on well with everyone he worked with; he was known as a big softy and was very loyal to everyone.

The séance: It was interesting to talk with Alan Rickman's spirit. He came across as very private, kind and humble, and the energy in the room was very calm. He was articulate and spoke ever so clearly with a distinctive voice, and he said he was happy to have a chat and to give us his time.

When we asked him about his career, he said he'd loved doing what he did, and his career had been the main part of his life for many years. He said he never left anything undone. He always worked hard and did a lot of research into his characters; he was a perfectionist and wanted them to appear in a certain way. He put all his effort into his roles and took his craft very seriously. In fact, his life had been dedicated to his craft.

He said his personal life was private, but he'd had a soulmate he adored very much. He'd liked to read a lot and loved to travel because it gave him the freedom to learn more about the world and the people in it. He had wanted to do more travelling because the world was such an interesting place. He also said he liked to keep things real, and, as a freethinker, didn't like any political rubbish from people. He'd loved his partner, his home and garden, and his simple but busy life.

WORDS OF WISDOM

Don't waste your time taking yourself seriously. It's a waste of time.

Actors are agents of change.

I think every relationship should have its own rules.

I believe in having empathy and kindness for everyone, not just some people.

Always stay grounded and focused; it's the only way to live your life.

Los Angeles is not a town of airheads. There is a great deal of wonderment there.

Seriously, you have to laugh sometimes; it's the best way to remedy a bad situation.

Mickey Rooney

Birthname: Joseph Yule Jr
Born: 23 September 1920, New York City, United States
Died: 6 April 2014, Los Angeles, California, United States – natural causes and diabetes complications.
Astrological sign: Libra
Day number 6: Gentle, caring, home lovers, compassionate, nurturing, family-oriented, magnetic personalities.

Mickey Rooney was a famous American actor and comedian from New York City, with a career spanning nearly nine decades. He appeared in over three hundred films and was one of the last surviving stars of the silent-film era. He was a small man, at only 152 centimetres tall. He first started his career in films at the age of six. He also worked in TV, radio and vaudeville.

He is best remembered for the Andy Hardy series, in which he worked as a child actor for the head of Metro-Goldwyn-Mayer, Louise B. Mayer. Mickey was a celebrated character actor and a famous figure across America. In his later years, he appeared as a guest actor on TV and appeared in many Broadway shows. Through his gambling and mismanagement of funds, he died broke and alienated from most of his family.

The séance: When Mickey came through, it was not in the usual séance, with all the sitters, but just after I'd finished a workout in my pool. This was when I was doing the experimental séance group and working with famous spirits. I thought to myself, this is interesting, no rest for the wicked, and I assumed he wanted to be in the group of famous spirit people, having heard about it through the spirit grapevine. There are always things going on when you work with spirit that often have no explanation, so you just learn to go with it.

I suddenly heard his voice in my ear, talking really fast, and I stopped what I was doing. He introduced himself and went on to talk about his life. He said he'd always given everything a go, no matter what the consequences were. Because he was short, he never liked to work with really tall actresses, but that didn't stop him from pursuing a successful career. He said he'd always been full of energy and had wanted to do so much with his life.

Romance and being in love were big on the agenda for him. He said it was always important to be in love, even though he may have picked the wrong person most of the time.

He said every single minute of his time had been spent thinking of new ideas, new films, different roles; his mind was always busy. His work was his passion, and nothing else mattered, but very unfortunately he'd got caught up too much in his own demons and problems.

When he finally came through in the group séance later that evening, he was like a dynamo. He told everyone, enthusiastically, that he loved women, had been married eight times, and had got on very well with his last wife, speaking very kindly about her. He also said that because of his short stature, he'd been hired to play a child even when he became older, which annoyed him.

He spoke very kindly of Judy Garland and said he'd loved to work with her, as they were great friends, unlike some of the women he'd been involved with.

Words of wisdom

I buy women shoes and they use them to walk away from me.

Always get married in the morning.

You always pass failure on your way to success.

I did not want to be short.

You've got to recognise there will never be another you.

I'm the only man in the world with a marriage licence made out to whom it may concern.

A lot of people have asked me how short I am.

Bon Scott

Birthname: Ronald Belford Scott
Born: 9 July 1946, Forfar, Scotland, United Kingdom
Died: 19 February 1980, East Dulwich, London, United Kingdom – acute alcohol poisoning.
Astrological sign: Cancer
Day number 9: Imaginative, passionate, creative, strong spiritual beliefs, like to run their own show, have trouble trusting, need to let go of things that no longer serve them.

Bon Scott was a well-loved Australian singer, songwriter and instrumentalist, famous both at home and internationally. For five years, he was the lead vocalist, lyricist and frontman for the great international Australian band AC/DC. With his bare chest, black hair, lewd manner, and big-larrikin personality, he was named the greatest rock frontman of all time in classic rock.

Bon, as he liked to be called, was originally from Forfar, Scotland, and moved with his family to Melbourne at the age of six, later settling in Fremantle, Western Australia. His death was a shock to everybody, friends and fans, as he was at the top of his career when he passed.

His friends often said Bon was a straight-up-and-down character and you knew exactly what he was thinking – that he was real, and as honest as the day is long. It's often said he will never be forgotten in the music industry.

The séance: When he came through in the séance and was asked by the control who he was, he answered with his name, and then there was silence for a while. We didn't understand why it took him a while to say more than his name, but when the lead control asked him a few more questions, he finally started talking.

He said he was remorseful about his death, as it had been a senseless accident and could have been avoided. He said several times he was annoyed at himself for the way he had died. He'd loved what he did and there'd been so much more he wanted to do. He'd loved being a front man and loved his job.

He talked about his music but seemed pretty upset. He kept saying he'd had no intention of going anywhere because he'd loved his work, but he knew that his addictions had taken over at times, like a dark cloud of demons and misery. He said he'd never had any control over these dark moods. He also berated himself for not having taken proper care of his health. He repeated often that he'd loved what he did and had been at the top of his career, enjoying life with his mates and going places.

He spoke about how much his music had meant to him, and how it had opened him up to so many experiences and adventures all over the world. He'd loved to entertain and could be 'a bit of a show-off', but he was happy doing this as it gave him so many opportunities to meet with people from all walks of life. He loved living the life of the true rock star, and he hadn't been ready to stop.

Words of wisdom

Always look after yourself and your health, and don't do rubbish.

It's all about living the dream and going for it. That way, nobody gets in the way.

Follow your heart and love, she'll never give up on you.

Not paying attention to red flags and other warnings around us telling us to stop and look at ourselves can often be dangerous.

Never give up.

Make sure you take control of your own life and don't depend on others, as often they won't be there.

Make sure you do it today, not later now.

Frank Sinatra

Born: 12 December 1915, Hoboken,
New Jersey, United States
Died: 14 May 1998, Los Angeles, California,
United States – heart attack.
Astrological sign: Sagittarius
Day number 3: Builders of the world, highly creative,
have an eye for beauty, hard workers.

Frank Sinatra was an Italian immigrant and well-known American singer and actor. His nicknames included Ol' Blue Eyes, The Voice, or Chairman of the Board. He was regarded as one of the most popular entertainers and musical artists of the 20th century, with sales of millions of records.

Frank began his career during the swing era and was highly successful, especially after going out on his own. He made his start as a big-band singer, then did really well with the Tommy Dorsey Orchestra from 1940 to 1942, which established him as a popular phenomenon and the biggest male singing star since Bing Crosby. Two of his big hits were 'Polka Dots and Moonbeams' and 'My Way'. He also had a highly successful acting career and received the Academy Award for Best Supporting Actor for *From Here to Eternity*. Besides singing and acting in sold-out theatres, he also worked on TV and kept winning awards.

Although he was married four times, his greatest love was Ava Gardner, the legendary actress. He confessed that he had been having a passionate affair with Ava while married to his first wife, Nancy, who he said he still loved in his own way. It's claimed that after seeing a photo of Ava in a magazine, he swore he would marry her. Although they eventually married, it didn't last long, and they remained friends. Nancy was the one ex-wife he kept in contact with throughout his life.

Frank had many friends throughout his life, including Elvis Presley, Dean Martin, Sammy Davis Jnr and John F Kennedy. Frank supported John Kennedy's presidential campaign, and brought Hollywood glamour to their friendship.

As a tough working-class Italian-American, Frank had friends and contacts in the Mafia; he liked to call them 'The boys'. He always denied this, but people who knew him offered their own proof. He was also a member of the Rat Pack, an informal group of singers and actors that included Frank Sinatra, Dean Martin, Joey Bishop, Peter Lawford, Sammy Davis Jr., and Shirley MacLaine – the only female member.

The séance: The night we were visited by Frank, the session didn't last too long. It was almost as if he didn't have a lot of time to spend with us. The group later said they felt he'd had no interest in what we were doing, for whatever reason. He seemed pleasant enough, but spoke very carefully through the medium, often taking his time.

When asked about his music, however, he spoke freely, became animated and even laughed. When we asked about the women in his life, he didn't say much other than he'd been devoted to his first wife, who was the mother of his children. He said he'd loved all his wives in his own way. They'd all been very different from one another, and he'd been a different person when he'd met each one of them.

He said he liked to call the shots, had never done anything he didn't want to do, was old-fashioned in some ways when it came to women, was big on people's loyalty or their word, and he'd had no time for people who were time-wasters or not straight with him. This would make him angry. He said singing and acting had been good for him, as he was able to express himself completely, free of any frustrations and shackles, and the rubbish that went on in the world. He also told us there'd been a lot of misinformation and gossip said about him, and he liked his privacy. This was something he kept repeating throughout the session.

When we asked him about Marilyn Monroe, he said nothing except she was a 'crazy mixed-up broad'. He wouldn't talk about the subject anymore and said it didn't interest him.

Words of wisdom

You only live once, and the way I live, once is enough.

The best revenge is success.

Alcohol may be man's worst enemy, but the Bible says love your money.

I'm trying to figure out, chairman of what board?

A friend is never an imposition.

The best is yet to come, and won't that be fun?

You only go around once, but if you play your cards right, once is enough.

Anna Nicole Smith

Birthname: Vickie Lynn Marshall
Born: 28 November 1967, in Houston, Texas, United States
Died: 8 February 2007, Hollywood, Florida, United States – accidental overdose of prescription drugs.
Astrological sign: Sagittarius
Day number 1: Born leaders, independent, ambitious, hardworking, prefer to work on their own rather than with others, can be stubborn.

Anna Nicole Smith was known to the world as a sexy American model, television personality and actress. She was also a *Playboy* centrefold and won the 1993 Playmate of the Year title. Her life was controversial, with plenty of drama. She died tragically from an accidental drug overdose, just as her beloved son Daniel Wayne Smith had, not long after the birth of her baby girl, Dannielynn Birkhead. She and her son were inseparable, and some say that because she had such a strong bond with her son, the timing was a tragic coincidence. After a DNA test, Dannielynn's biological father was granted sole custody of their daughter. Anna's legacy lives on through her daughter.

She was renowned for films like *The Naked Gun* and *The Final Insult* and was given her own reality show on cable network, which achieved the highest rating for a reality show. She was also known for the drama involving her late husband's multimillion-dollar estate. Anna lost her claim to any portion of the Marshall estate, and all funds were left to the Marshall family.

The séance: When Anna Nicole came into the séance, her energy was very fast, and when asked if she had anything to say through the medium, she spoke very briefly about her family. She said it had been everything she cherished in the world, by far the most important thing in her life. All the sitters commented it was if she was on a mission. We could all feel her energy as she manifested in the room and went around the circle.

When she settled, she began to speak through me, the medium. She came across as a gentle, kind and sensitive soul, and spoke in a soft voice. She said she had loved attention and being in the limelight, but on a personal level, unfortunately real love had eluded her for most of her short life, and she'd felt lonely a lot of the time. She'd always felt like an outsider.

Anna Nicole said she'd grown tired of people always thinking they knew her and constantly judging her. All she'd wanted was to be loved, respected and understood. She'd loved entertaining people and liked to see them pay attention and laugh, even though she could see through most of them.

She said it had been good to be reunited with her son after his death. She'd felt whole again. They had been what she called 'soulmates', and she believed they'd shared a special bond. She said she had been sad to lose her daughter, who was left behind. Then she laughed and said that her daughter, who looked like her, would give all those around her a run for their money because she was so smart.

Anna Nicole said she knew she would always be remembered, and it made her happy to know her life had impacted people, because she had always wanted to be famous.

WORDS OF WISDOM

Just do the best you can. Be you. You know how to.

Always love yourself and understand how important that is. Self-love is a state of appreciation for yourself that grows from actions that support your physical, psychological and spiritual growth.

Love yourself first and others will love you, too, in return.

Pay attention to your own sensitivities and needs as they will always need work; boundaries are an integral part of life.

Be aware of toxic patterns, and people who may abuse your fragile spirit.

Have a high regard for your own happiness, family and wellbeing.

Stop sabotaging your life by putting others' needs first and pleasing others, as boundaries are essential in your life.

Doris Stokes

Born: 6 January 1920, Lincolnshire,
England, United Kingdom
Died: 8 May 1987, Lewisham, London,
England, United Kingdom – cancer.
Astrological sign: Capricorn
Day number 6: Gentle, caring, home lovers, compassionate, nurturing, family orientated, magnetic personalities.

Doris May Fisher Stokes was a British spiritualist, professional medium and author of many books. In her memoirs, she claimed she started seeing spirits and hearing disembodied voices in childhood, and she developed these abilities further once she joined a local spiritualist church, after her son died in infancy. She was well known in the world and was an inspiration to many aspiring mediums.

Besides mediumship—working mainly with clairaudience, or clear hearing in mediumship—she described her gift as being like talking to someone on a phone. She did spirit rescues with other mediums to release earthbound spirits from homes and buildings. She often told stories of her spirit children, and helped many people believe in the work of a medium, as she brought joy and healing to so many.

Her public performances, TV appearances and memoirs made her a household name in Britain, and also in Australia, where she appeared on the *Don Lane Show*. While in Australia, she filled the Sydney Opera House and was mobbed in the streets.

Sadly, her health was poor throughout her life; she had thirteen cancer operations, including a mastectomy, and did not regain consciousness after an operation to remove a brain tumour.

The séance: It was no surprise when Doris finally came into the spirit séance one night as, being a big fan, I was half expecting it. I had read all her books when I was a young student. She was always in the background after she died, and to this day I'm convinced she worked with me many times in my own public stage shows.

All the sitters were thrilled, as well, and I could hear them chatting happily amongst themselves when she came through my channel. Before long, I could hear the control asking Doris questions about herself. Then I sensed a breeze all around us, building slowly and then getting stronger. It was spirit energy coming into the small circle very quickly.

The control soon stopped talking and, through me, Doris asked each person if they wanted a reading or a message from a loved one. She said she wasn't there to talk about herself but was more interested in helping every single person in the room. We went around the circle, and one by one, I could feel her talking through me, using her voice box and giving every single person a reading from a loved one.

I have always loved Doris Stokes's work. She has been like a spiritual mentor, not only for me, but also for so many other fellow mediums who walk this often-difficult path. For so many years, the words in her books, which are very kind and healing, gave me so much comfort and support. She has always been an inspiration, helping me keep going. It was interesting to feel her energy as she came across as so humble and motherly. Nothing seemed to be a problem, and I could feel my heart chakra expanding as I gave the messages to the sitters in the room.

In my own spiritual development over the years, Doris and her spiritual guide—Romanov, a Tibetan monk—have given me the inspiration to work hard with my own abilities. The faith and guidance I've received in trance and meditation has been wonderful, as one needs a lot of faith when working as a medium, especially when working with the public, which can at times be challenging.

I don't know how many times over the years I have read Doris's books, like so many others, just for comfort, and it often felt like she was in the room with me. In her books, she wrote about little spirit lights in her audience bopping around the intended person she was to read for. I haven't experienced that, but I have worked with her spiritual guide many times. Doris loved not so much talking as working.

Words of wisdom

Keep the faith and always believe in spirit as you will always be looked after.

Know when it's your time to help humanity, as the world needs you now.

Don't be afraid of what you can do with your psychic gifts. They're always changing anyway, and your spirit team is always there by your side to guide and protect you. You are never alone.

Once the spirit energy is inside you, the body can do anything. When I worked, I was never sick. It was only when the spirit energy left.

Don't forget to always ask for help from your spirit team. They are there for a reason. All you have to do is listen.

Love and forgiveness are the greatest healing tools in the world. When you learn to use them, your days are brighter.

Just because they say they're spiritual doesn't mean they are. I was never a fan of big groups, not for a long time, anyway. I loved to work with my own spirit team.

Gloria Swanson

Born: 27 March 1899, Chicago, Illinois, United States
Died: 4 April 1983, New York City, United States – heart failure.
Astrological sign: Aries
Day number 9: Imaginative, passionate, creative, strong, have spiritual beliefs, like to run their own show, have trouble trusting, need to let go of the things that no longer serve them.

Gloria Swanson was a glamorous, famous Hollywood star, producer and inventor. She was one of the biggest, most successful and highest-paid stars of her time, starring in dozens of silent films and working with the legendary director, Cecil B DeMille. She was nominated for the first Academy Award. She was also one of the first women in history to produce her own films.

In 1929, Gloria transitioned into the 'talkies' and later, after a lull in her career, ventured into television and theatre. She was also known for her outstanding dress sense and extravagant style. This was a woman who shone very brightly in the world with her creative flair. She was nominated three times for the Academy Award for Best Actress and became famous for her 1959 turn as the fading movie queen Norma Desmond in Billy Wilder's *Sunset Boulevard*, a role that earned her a Golden Globe Award. Her favourite leading man in 'talkies' was William Holden.

She wrote a book, published by Random House, claiming she'd had a three-year love affair with Joseph P Kennedy. During her company's existence, she also helped develop a carbide-steel alloy cutting tool and developed the first plastic buttons for clothing. It was also Gloria's company that invented the extension cord. As a Republican, she was head of the council for Seniors for Reagan–Bush.

The séance: We were thrilled when Gloria came into the séance. We all felt her regal energy, and it was obvious that she must have been a big personality in her day, a woman of substance who knew what she wanted and how to get it. She had a very strong presence and sophisticated, big energy.

When the sitters spoke to her, through me, she spoke in a matter-of-fact manner, but in a soft tone. She told us she had always been interested in the occult and spiritual matters, and was big on manifesting her desires through philosophies she had studied while alive. She'd spent a large portion of her life using these techniques to achieve what she wanted to do with creative projects.

I've always been a fan of Gloria Swanson, from my early days. I believed she was a true artist, a trendsetter in what I would call 'a man's world'. I was always inspired by her and took an interest in her acting career, lifestyle, fashion, the way she went about things, and how she managed to do so much for a woman of her era.

She spoke about how important it was to give to children's charities, as children are the new leaders of the world. She said every child needs to feel safe and have love and support in their life.

WORDS OF WISDOM

Don't follow the sheep; be sassy and a true leader.

Sometimes in life we can have so many difficult challenges. In this case, don't rush forward, go around.

This untimely message today is a reminder that no matter how difficult or frustrating you find the situation to be, or how many endless blocks appear on your journey, have patience, as all will soon pass.

Once you move on with your success, it will just be another experience to put under your belt. Be courageous and know all is well.

I love to eat healthy good food. Especially if it's organic and raw. It works for my mind, emotions and body.

Be realistic and always live in the present, not the past or future.

Make sure you're the best in everything you do. I always did, and I loved what I did with a passion.

Tina Turner

Birthname: Anna Mae Bullock
Born: 26 November 1939, Brownsville, Tennessee, United States
Died: 24 May 2023, Kusnacht, Switzerland – cancer, stroke and kidney failure.
Astrological sign: Sagittarius
Day number 8: Good businesspeople, know how to make money, self-confident, need to be careful when selecting partners.

Tina Turner was an iconic American-born Swiss singer, actress and songwriter, known famously as the Queen of Rock and Roll. Tina began singing as a teenager and, after moving to St. Louis, Missouri, she immersed herself in the local rhythm-and-blues scene. She met Ike Turner at a performance by his band, the Kings of Rhythm, and became part of the act. Her electric performance and stage presence quickly made her the centrepiece of the band.

After divorcing Ike after years of abuse, she made a comeback on her own and became an enormous star in the 1980s. With her incredible gravelly voice, sensuality, star power and rock-and-roll swagger, she was an incredible force.

Over the years, she sold 150 million records as a recording artist, won twelve Grammy Awards, and was inducted into the Grammy Hall of Fame. She was known for many songs, including 'What's Love Got to Do with It', which made her a superstar, and 'Proud Mary'.

The séance: Imagine my surprise when, not long after she died, the spirit of Tina came to me in a meditation, rather than the usual séance. As I sat in my space, I could hear her laughing loudly in her deep voice as she came into the room, with one of her songs blasting in the background. I felt like I had electricity in my body, as her energy was so powerful. It made me realise that Tina had been put on Earth to do great work in the time she was here. I was also not surprised to be working with her, as she was a legend and someone I have admired for so long, as a woman and a performer. The spirit world always has ways of making things happen.

When she came through, Tina talked about how much she'd loved performing. It had been like therapy for her, she said, as her life had not been easy and her work had given her a whole lot of love, satisfaction and deep healing on a soul level. The suffering she'd endured was made up for by her ability to sing and perform to heal people on a soul level.

She also spoke about how she loved to work with other musicians sometimes as it was fun, and she was happy to learn, share and teach her knowledge. Tina also spoke about her family and loved ones, and how very special they were to her, and how they'd kept her going. She was also very grateful to able to be with her soulmate, her husband, who had supported and loved her deeply.

Tina had been through so much in her life, and she said it was her belief that nothing is impossible when you put your mind to it, but it's also important to have the right connections. Her creative spirit was with her right to the end and still lives on in our hearts.

Words of Wisdom

My greatest beauty secret is to be happy with myself. I don't use special creams or treatment; I use a bit of everything.

Sometimes you've got to let everything go, purge yourself.

My legacy is that I stayed on course, from the beginning to the end, because I believed in something inside of me.

I believe that if you'll just stand up and go, life will open up for you.

I'm the only person left doing the kind of work that I do.

The real power behind whatever success I have now was something I found within myself, something that is in all of us.

I will never give in to old age until I become old. And I'm not old yet.

Paul Walker

Born: 12 September 1973, Glendale, California, United States
Died: 30 November 2013, Santa Clarita, California, United States – car crash.
Astrological sign: Virgo
Day number 3: Builders of the world, highly creative, have an eye for beauty, hard workers.

Paul Walker started his career as a child actor. An American actor, he appeared in *The Young and the Restless* but was best known as Brian O'Connor of the *Fast & Furious* franchise, which became famous around the world because of its off-beat modern culture. His death was a great tragedy for everyone who knew him, including the crew of the franchise and the actors with whom he had worked for many years.

Paul also worked as a presenter for the marine biology series *Expedition Great White,* and became known for his philanthropic efforts, founding the disaster-relief charity Reach Out Worldwide.

When Paul died, he was a passenger in a Porsche driven by his friend Roger Rodas, who lost control of the car; both men were killed. The coroner said they were travelling at over one hundred miles per hour when the car crashed and burst into flames. Paul's entire estate was left to his daughter and only child, who was only fifteen at the time. Vin Diesel, Paul's close friend, is the godfather of Paul's daughter.

The séance: I can honestly say I had no idea of who this young actor was when he came through in the group séance one night. The spirit control told us it was Paul Walker who brought the spirit children to the séances each time, and we were all surprised by this, but it made sense later when Paul told us he liked fast cars, like the spirit boy, Johnny.

Over time, Paul dropped in a few times, and he always came across as a very kind soul, quite spiritual, and it was lovely the way he spoke fondly of his daughter, who he missed greatly. He also mentioned he was saddened by his crash. Friendships had meant a lot to him when he was alive, he said. He was sad at his death because he'd had so much more to do; when he died things had been going really well for him in his acting career.

Not long after his untimely arrival, I started seeing Paul everywhere—late at night on TV and in his movies—but I had no idea who he was. Perhaps he wanted to be remembered, like the other spirits that have come to our private séances over the years.

The funny thing is that after a while, one of the spirit children, Johnny, took a fancy to Paul, and often said at the beginning of a séance that Paul had brought him and the kids in from the spirit world 'in his nice car'. Johnny had told us how much he loves fast and fancy cars and was excited to arrive from the spirit world in this way. I still have no idea why the spirit children get Paul to drive them. It remains a mystery to this day.

Words of Wisdom

Make the most of everything in your life, as it goes by very quickly sometimes.

It's not about working anymore; it's about doing work I can be proud of.

I live by, 'Go big or go home.'

I like a woman who is capable and at the same time feminine.

The dream is to have it all.

Sometimes the hurdles aren't really hurdles at all.

Well done is better than well said.

Shane Warne

Born: 13 September 1969, Upper Ferntree Gully, Victoria, Australia
Died: 4 March 2022, Ko Samui, Thailand – heart attack.
Astrological sign: Virgo
Day number 4: Down to earth, have difficulty making decisions, honest and trustworthy.

Shane Warne was an Australian icon, a well-loved character. He was known as a right-arm leg-spin bowler and batsman from Victoria. In his career as an Australian and international cricket player, he was regarded as one of the sport's greatest ever bowlers. He, unlike some, never gave up on his sport. He revolutionised cricket-related thinking, with his mastery of the leg spin, which had come to be regarded as a dying art.

After his retirement, Shane was kept busy as a TV and radio commentator, and through his work with charitable organisations. He was given a State memorial, and a statue of him bowling was placed outside the Melbourne Cricket Ground.

The séance: When Shane came into the séance, he came across as very humble, sad then happy. He said he wasn't happy about the way he had died, and if he'd had things his way, he would've loved to stay around longer; he'd had unfinished business and so much more living to do.

When asked about his sport, he said he'd loved and lived for his sport ever since he could remember. It had opened so many doors and given him opportunities he could never have dreamt of. Laughing, he went on to say that his biggest mistake had been thinking he was immortal. He often burned the candle at both ends, and at times never felt well. This was because he had what he said was nervous energy. He wanted to do the many things this nervous energy wanted him to do.

As a group, we thought he was confused about his death. He kept repeating that he'd had no idea he was going to die so young; he hadn't been ready. He'd had so much more life to live. He said he thought he got food poisoning. He was aware that he'd had a heart issue but felt that it wouldn't be a problem and so did not take responsibility.

He also said that having children was another of his accomplishments and he loved them all dearly. At the time of his death, he had met somebody he cared about. He'd loved to be loved; he'd been a true romantic in the love department.

Before he left, he kept saying he loved his family, he was sorry, and he was grateful for everything that had happened to him.

Words of wisdom

To me, cricket is a simple game. Keep it simple and just go out and play.

You can't afford to live your life with regrets.

I am no dummy, mate, that's for sure.

I'm proud of what I've achieved in cricket, as once I didn't think I was good enough.

We've just got to be careful with all sports and not just cricket. I think there's so much emphasis on doing the right thing all the time, but I think the public want to be entertained when they come to watch sport.

I just play because I love playing, and I try and take as many wickets as I can.

I've always tried to move on from disappointments as fast as I can.

Dame Vivienne Westwood

Birthname: Vivienne Isabel Swire
Born: 8 April 1941, Cheshire, England, United Kingdom
Died: 29 December 2022, London, England, United Kingdom – peacefully, surrounded by family.
Astrological sign: Aries
Day number 8: Good businesspeople, know how to make money, self-confident, need to be careful when selecting partners.

Dame Vivienne Westwood was a famous fashion designer and businesswoman. One of the most influential designers of the 20th century and icon to many, she was affectionately known as the High Priestess of Punk and the Queen of Extreme. She was very creative, and right up until her death was known to push the boundaries of the industry. She received the Order of the British Empire from the Queen in 1992 and made the front cover of *Tatler* magazine. She had an odd and wild character, and it was said that she didn't care what people thought. Because of her success in fashion, she became a national treasure.

Vivienne was also involved artistically with the English punk rock band the Sex Pistols, helping develop the visual grammar of the punk movement, alongside their manager, Malcom McLaren. The Sex Pistols created a revolution in the music world. The band changed the genre of music forever in the 1970s and early 1980s. She also changed women's fashion by designing frocks for women who had breasts and hips.

The séance: I have followed Vivienne for a long time as I was a fan of the Sex Pistols in the 1970s and saw them a few times when living overseas. She was an icon in her day, an amazing artist, and I was thrilled when she came through.

As I began to blend my energies with hers, I could hear her laughing and talking in my ear in a curious way. She thought the whole process was amusing and said she'd always had a fascination with the supernatural. This was good news to me, so I relaxed more and could really feel her quirky, restless energy. Her spirit was curious, and I realised she must have had a lot of energy in her day.

She spoke about how she'd always liked to shake things up, and I saw her as a naughty pixie, especially the way she talked about her work, which had been her life. I feel that making statements to shock people may have been a front, because I sensed in real life, she had been very private, almost like having two types of personalities.

She said that she'd been unwell for a while before her death, almost as if all the energy or life stream was running out of her body. It was a shame she died when she did, because she was a visionary, with so much still to do. I'm sure she'll be still working long hours in the spirit world. She also spoke about past lifetimes in France and England, and being involved in the royal courts.

WORDS OF WISDOM

If you're going to do something, do it properly. Make a statement.

It's not possible for a man to be elegant without a touch of femininity.

I'm in my own head most of the time.

I'm the proof that you can't throw away tradition.

The only possible effect one can have on the world is through unpopular ideas.

My aim is to make the poor look rich and the rich look poor.

Fashion is very important; it's life enhancing and, like everything that gives pleasure, it's worth doing well.

Betty White

Birthname: Betty Marion Ludden
Born: 17 January 1922, Oak Park, Illinois, United States
Died: 31 December 2021, Los Angeles, California, United States –natural causes.
Astrological sign: Capricorn
Day number 8: Good businesspeople, know how to make money, self-confident, need to be careful when selecting partners.

Betty White was an American treasure. She was best known for her comedic work in numerous TV sitcoms, including *The Mary Tyler Moore Show* and *The Golden Girls*. Her career spanned decades, but she considered her marriage to her third husband, Alan Ludden, among her greatest accomplishments. She was also known for her kindness, which was consistent in all her memorable roles, and she was loved by so many people, including fans, family and friends.

She worked with animal rights and had supported the Morris Animal Foundation since the 1970s, where she campaigned for health studies with dogs, cats, lizards and wildlife. She was also known for her kindness, which was consistent in all her memorable roles, and she was loved by so many people, including fans, family and friends.

The séance: I'm sure Betty was really nice in life as she was delightful in spirit. Everyone in the room loved her kind and hilarious energy, and everyone clapped when she left the room. She had such a big energy and a fast mind, considering she was such a tiny woman, and came across as a straightshooter. The funniest thing was, instead of us asking her the questions, she kept asking us things, like, hysterically, why we were sitting in the dark.

To my surprise, Betty's energy and compassion was very similar to Doris Day's; when Doris came through years ago, it was obvious she loved animals as much as Betty. It was no surprise that everyone's passed-over pets came into the séance.

This was the first time I had brought the spirit of a snake to a séance. Little did I know that one of the sitters had a pet snake that had passed, and she got a shock when the snake came in and said hello through the medium, which was me. I had never communicated with a snake before, so I guess that was Betty's naughty sense of humour. After all, she had been a big animal lover in life and still is in the spirit world.

Before she went, Betty said she was happy to have lived a long life and was very grateful for the opportunities she'd had as an actress. She also said she liked to look nice, with her hair done, wearing nice clothes and makeup.

Words of wisdom

I'm not into animal rights. I'm only into animal welfare and health.

I'm not what you call sexy, I'm a romantic. Let's put it that way.

I may be a senior, but so what? I'm still hot.

I have a two-storey house and a bad memory, so I'm up and down those stairs all the time.

I didn't know what Facebook was, and now that I do know what it is, I have to say it sounds interesting.

I was an only child, and I had a mother and father... They were fun and we would laugh a lot.

I make it my business to get along with people so I can have fun. It's that simple.

CONCLUSION – THE MEDIUM IN A MODERN WORLD

As a naturally eager student of spiritualism from the age of seventeen, I have always been interested in and deeply involved with occultism and the pursuit of truth beyond the visible world, and the mysterious forces guiding a soul's journey. I'm also drawn to the theosophical doctrine promoted by Helen Blavatsky and the 'tenet of the universal brotherhood of humanity'.

Working between two worlds as a spiritual medium for most of my life, I can certainly say that in my private séances and readings with people, it has been a wild ride—very entertaining, educational and memorable, to say the least.

When I first started out with my experimental séances, I had no idea I would be talking and communicating with not just loved ones in the spirit world, who have safely crossed beyond the veil for sitters and clients, but also famous personalities.

I see all of this as a healing process, as it's all about these spirits leaving their legacies to help us on our own paths. While under in the trance state, I would listen to the information, and sometimes I could not believe all the information I channelled through to the group energy. It made me realise these icons were once ordinary people, but they were able to fly and reach the top of their field, a reminder that anything is possible if you believe in yourself and give it a go.

I would also like to mention that all the spirits who came through have passed safely into the spirit world, and I have been given permission from them to share all their beautiful messages. Talk about starstruck. In fact, the messages of love we all received during every evening we sat were very uplifting and special. It was if we were all given personal insights into their private lives, which was very soulful and inspiring.

The strangest thing was that with every sitting over the many years, nothing was ever planned. For example, I never had any idea exactly which spirit was going to drop in. We just opened the circle and left it all up to my trusted spirit team.

After we closed down on each occasion, one of the sitters would write down everything after a group discussion, and some of the sitters would do the research and check all the information to see if it made sense and was true. The information we received was incredible, and we were all excited to be a part of it.

A message I have channelled from my guide, White Feather:

'As the world races ahead of us with so many changes in technology, politics, wars, religion, the environment and ideologies, every single one of us needs help, assistance, guidance and inspiration in our daily lives.

'On reflection, all these experiences we go through every day, are all part of our spiritual contracts and the journey we all signed up for. Yes, it can at times be a bumpy road less travelled, with often challenging and difficult experiences along the way, but it makes us who we are today.

'The good thing is that through our intention with prayer, meditation or simple requests, which are direct links to the spirit world, we will always receive assistance, as we are always heard, with loving messages from the spirit world.

'Believe in miracles always, as they do exist and can happen every day, as we are never alone, not for one minute. Keep the faith, because just knowing this is a healing in itself, and always be your authentic self, as others see your light.'

AFTERWORD

Spirit people always say they're no longer in their old earthbound bodies, and are young again, without being hindered by any type of disease or illness that they may once have suffered on Earth. Just because there may have been a suicide or terrible death, it does not mean the soul stays stuck in the astral.

Once we've made the transition into spirit, as a soul in a spirit body, we no longer need to eat, we appear younger and we are blessed, as we are accompanied by loved ones, pets and old friends who have passed on as well.

The process is described as beautiful, providing the spirit with a sense of elation and a complete feeling of total peace. After crossing over, all spirits spend time assessing the many spiritual lessons they learned during their time on Earth – healing, learning and growing further as they receive a life review from advanced souls in the spirit world.

Souls who have suffered painful deaths will spend time in the place of oneness, which can be described as 'the spirit hospital'. Once this process is completed, the soul once again returns to their soul groups, depending on how well they have learned their lessons, returning to their true essence until reincarnation.

Always know the spirits of your loved ones, from generations past, are around you, supporting you and continuing to love you always. They will also be there to greet you when you have completed your karmic cycle on Earth, and they will help you cross as you shed your human form and once again return to spirit, your true form.

I hope you have enjoyed the experience of meeting these beautiful souls as much as my sitters and I have. It was a wonderful experience, to say the least, and it brought us so much joy and wonderment. These highly inspirational souls did the journey on Earth their way. The gift they have given us is to inspire us to believe in our dreams, be original and go for what we want in our lives.

I feel so humbled to share this information with the world, and as a student of spirit, all I can say is anything is possible when you believe in yourself and open your heart to spirit. I love my work as a medium and feel grateful to share my gifts with you, as anything is possible in the big scheme of things.

My main abilities are that of a mental medium, but as a passionate student of spirit, I'm willing to constantly learn new things, as it has been my life's work.

Throughout the years, I have sat in many groups and run many of my own. To date, I am trained in trance mediumship, physical mediumship, spirit rescue, spiritual healing and spiritual regression work. I have been sitting in my own closed physical group and séances, which I call my experimental group, which is closed to the public.

I am still, to this day, very humbled and grateful to have had this type of experience.

Love, light and many blessings on your path.

RECOMMENDED READING

Blavatsky, Helen. *The Secret Doctrine.* The Theosophical Publishing Company (London), 1888.

Blavatsky, Helen. *Isis Unveiled.* Theosophical Society (United States), 1877.

Blavatsky, Helen. *The Key to Theosophy.* The Theosophical Publishing Company (London), 1889.

Cannon, Dolores. *Between Life and Death: Conversations with Spirit.* Ozark Mountain Publishing, 2103.

Erwin, Kerrie. *A Medium's Story.* Amazon, 2024.

Erwin, Kerrie. *Celebrity Oracle.* Rockpool Publishing, November 2023.

Erwin, Kerrie. *Spirit Rescue.* Llewellyn Publishing, April 2023.

Erwin, Kerrie. *Mediumship.* Rockpool Publishing, 2021.

Erwin, Kerrie. *Clearing.* Rockpool Publishing, 2020.

Erwin, Kerrie. *Sacred Signs.* Rockpool Publishing, 2017.

Erwin, Kerrie. *Sacred Space.* Feng Shui-Rockpool Publishing, 2016.

Erwin, Kerrie. *Sacred Soul.* Rockpool Publishing, 2015.

Erwin, Kerrie. *Learning to Work with the Tarot.* Cards-Balboa, 2013.

Erwin, Kerrie. *Spirits Whispering in My Ear.* White Feather Publishing, 2012.

Erwin, Kerrie. *Memoirs of a Suburban Medium.* White Feather Publishing, 2011.

Erwin, Kerrie. *Magical Tales of the Forest.* White Feather Publishing, 2010.

Foy, Robin. *Witnessing the Impossible: The Skole Experiment.* Published in: *Proceedings of the Society for Psychical Research, 1999.*

Goodchild, Claire. *The Book of Séances.* Voracious (Hachette Book Group), 2022.

Morton, Lisa. *Calling the Spirits: A History of Séances.* Reaktion Books, 2020.

Newton, Michael. *Journey of Souls.* Llewellyn Publications, 1994.

Roland, Paul. *Explore Your Past Lives.* Godsfield Press, 2005.

ABOUT THE AUTHOR

With a nursing, teaching, performing arts, writing, and musical background, Sydney-based international medium Kerrie Erwin has lived between two worlds since childhood and can see and hear spirit people talking. With many years of training in spiritual studies, having joined the spiritual church at seventeen, she is a mental medium, trance medium, physical medium, and rescue medium.

With her spirit gifts, she could see and hear spirit people as a small child. After a near-death experience in her early twenties, she began working professionally as an energy worker, specialising in spiritual mediumship, trance, physical mediumship, and clairvoyance, focusing on spirit rescue, hauntings, and connecting people to loved ones who have passed over into the spirit world.

She has taught mediumship and metaphysics for many years, reads tarot cards and works with Feng Shui. Kerrie is also trained in spiritual hypnotherapies and past-life regression.

She is also a published author of twelve books to date and has written articles for magazines as a freelance writer.

In 2024, Kerrie's book, *A Medium's Story*, won the NYC Big Book Award in the spirituality section. The book offers readers a genuine glimpse into her life as a medium, sharing all the highs and lows and leaving them enthralled.

Kerrie works with *The Kerrie Erwin Spiritual Show*, a successful stage show that regularly tours Australia's clubs and venues, and also works extensively in radio and TV.

Kerrie also has a free segment on social media; her 'Kerrie Erwin: Public Figure' Facebook page offers free messages and spiritual advice, helping the community.

Kerrie Erwin, spiritual medium, clairvoyant and author
www.pureview.com.au

www.ingramcontent.com/pod-product-compliance
Lightning Source LLC
Chambersburg PA
CBHW042114100526
44587CB00025B/4043